that's just
MOISHE

Collected Wisdom, Wit and Whimsy from
the Founder of Jews for Jesus

that's just
MOISHE

Collected Wisdom, Wit and Whimsy from
the Founder of Jews for Jesus

Edited by Ruth Rosen

JEWS F✡R JESUS®
San Francisco, CA

Acknowledgments

Thanks to David Brickner, who wanted to share these letters, lessons and little sayings with you, and who came up with the title for this book; thanks to Susan Perlman for lending her keen eye for detail to this project; thanks to Josh Cohen, who went through many piles of manuscripts to find some of the lessons and little sayings; thanks to David Yapp for applying his considerable design and art skills, and to Amer Olson for giving us a wonderful portrait of Moishe for the cover. Thanks to Carol Clemons for capturing the whimsical side of Moishe, and of life in general. Thanks to God for Moishe Rosen, and his time on this earth from 1932–2010. And Dad, thanks for all that you taught me, and so many, many others. As packed as this book is with your wisdom, wit and whimsy, it only begins to scratch the surface.

To friends of Moishe
who miss his voice and words of wisdom:
may this book encourage your hearts and your walk with the One
in whose service these letters, lessons and little sayings
were written.

*That's Just Moishe: Collected Wisdom, Wit and Whimsy
from the Founder of Jews for Jesus*
Edited by Ruth Rosen

©2013 by Purple Pomegranate Productions
A division of JEWS F✡R JESUS®

Cover and book design: David Yapp
Cover illustration: Amer Olson
Inside illustrations and cartoons: Carol Clemons

All rights reserved. Nothing in this book shall be reprinted or reproduced, electronically or in any other manner, without express written permission.

All Scripture quoted, unless otherwise noted, is from the HOLY BIBLE, NEW INTERNATIONAL VERSION®. Copyright © 1973, 1978, 1984 Biblica. Used by permission of Zondervan. All rights reserved.

For more information, including reprint permission, contact:
JEWS F✡R JESUS®
60 Haight Street
San Francisco, CA 94102
USA

jewsforjesus.org
jfj@jewsforjesus.org

ISBN 10: 1-881022-97-8
ISBN 13: 978-1-881022-97-8

Contents

Foreword 9
by David Brickner, executive director

Part One: Letters 13
Love in Action 15
The Comfortable Cross 19
Unholy Tolerance 25
Liberty and Law..31
The Trouble You Need 37
Church Giving vs Missionary Giving...41
Curiosity Or 45
The Disintegrated Personality 49
On the Cutting Edge..53
Enduring..57
God is Not a Sourpuss...61
Of Mice and Birds..65

Part Two: Lessons 69
Brief topical excerpts arranged alphabetically 71
Additional lessons by page
    The Benefits of Praise 127
    Calvary: a Dark Image that Sheds Light.............................129
    Common Leadership Problems 131
    Spiritual Agriculture..133
    Commitment...135
    Faithfulness 139
    Dealing with Fear 141
    Spiritual Swordsmanship..143
    Value Judgments: What Is the Basis for
    "Ought" and "Ought Not" 145
    Why Witness to Jewish People?...149

Part Three: Little Sayings...153
Topics arranged alphabetically

Foreword

That's Just Moishe will give you a peek into the life and thinking of one of the most fascinating Jewish followers of Jesus since the Apostle Paul. A brilliant eccentric with a big belly and an even bigger heart, Moishe remained an enigma to many—but not to those of us who knew him best and loved him the most.

We wanted you to know more about Moishe than would fit into his compelling biography, *Called to Controversy*. We wanted you to hear his voice, to grasp some of his incisive thinking and to enjoy his unique sense of humor; hence this companion volume.

Moishe was always ready with a witty quip, and I wish we had written them all down. But those found in this volume reflect the *seychel* (wisdom) of this "homely sage" (that was his chosen "persona," the image that he felt best suited his informal speaking style).

Moishe often appeared to live somewhere in between his own thoughts and the world around him. As a result, he sometimes seemed less than aware of things others might notice, including his own appearance. He relied on close friends and family members to remind him to comb his hair or wipe that kernel of corn off his mustache. And his awareness of the road—well, if you could help it, you never wanted to be in the car when Moishe was driving. He would lean back with one hand on the wheel and look at you and talk and talk, all the while you were wide-eyed, staring at the road and barely able to converse for fear of your life. I am quite sure God routinely stationed extra angels on the hood of Moishe's car.

And yet, Moishe was also keenly aware and almost prophetically alert, with an ability to size up people and situations like no one else I have ever met. Once, as a new leader in our Jews for Jesus Chicago branch, I carefully prepared for a visit from Moishe. The office was spic-and-span. Everything was in its place, or so I thought. Moishe came into the office, immediately walked straight over to a stack of papers on top of a file cabinet and picked up a couple dozen documents. "What are these?" he asked. I didn't know. "These documents should have been entered into the computer two weeks ago." He was, of course, correct. It was uncanny. But that was just Moishe.

Yet because Moishe *could* sometimes be so absentminded, he was fun to "prank" (and, as a player of practical jokes himself, he was fair game). One of Moishe's mannerisms was to rub his tummy in a slow, circular motion as he spoke. It was a habit that was somewhat endearing. Once, Tuvya Zaretsky and I decided to play a little prank on him—an experiment really. We placed a rather large pumpkin on an end table right next to the chair Moishe would sit in to teach at our Tuesday Bible study. Moishe eyed the pumpkin several times in the first minute or two of the study, then slowly began to rub the pumpkin instead of his tummy. He continued to rub that pumpkin off and on through the entire Bible study! Tuvya and I stood in the back laughing silently, but so hard that tears were streaming down our faces. And that, too, was just Moishe.

I shed many more tears when Moishe announced that he was stepping down from his position as executive director—but those were tears of a different kind. The unique privilege of being mentored and led by this soft-spoken giant genius was drawing to an end, and he still had so much to give. If I have any regrets about Moishe, it is that the last years of his life were limited by his declining health. I wish he had written more, traveled more, taught more in his later years. But we still have a rich body of Moishe's teachings from when he was in full swing—and you'll find a good selection of them right here.

Foreword

So for those of you who have the capacity to recognize the gift, here is a bit more to love and a bit more to appreciate about the man named Moishe Rosen, the founder of Jews for Jesus, and someone very dear to my heart.

David Brickner, executive director
Jews for Jesus

THAT'S JUST MOISHE

Letters

These letters were originally addressed to all who receive the *Jews for Jesus Newsletter*. Moishe considered it a great privilege to write his monthly reflections to friends of our ministry.

His opening thoughts often served as an overarching perspective to the rest of our newsletter, adding insight to reports of our missionaries' adventures. But Moishe also wrote in an almost pastoral tone to address the needs of our readers. He wrote to inspire, ignite and sometimes challenge readers about what God wants to do—not only in and through Jews for Jesus—but in the hearts and lives of all believers.

We hope these letters will give you a lift!

Note: *With more than 200 letters to choose from, these twelve represent the editor's top picks, most of which were written in the 1980s. Most of the rest are available on our website (along with those you are about to read) at* jewsforjesus.org/articles-by-moishe.

Love in Action

Some say that the way to win people to the Lord is to "love them to Jesus." I don't like being aggressive. I like behaving toward others in a way that will help them like me. I would rather love people than shove them. (Of course, no one ever shoves anyone to Jesus. That shove—or gentler nudge, as the case may be—can only come from the moving of the Holy Spirit in a person's life.) Yet something is dramatically wrong with the "love them to Jesus" approach to evangelism.

The problem is human nature. We humans just don't do things as well as God does. In His absolute ability to express His love for the world, God sent Jesus to die on the cross. Certainly God is more competent than I—and if God's supreme act of love does not move some people toward Him, how can my puny affection succeed?

True love—God's agape love—contains no ulterior motives and no hidden agendas. It is not a means to an end, but an end in itself. It is a goal we believers try to achieve as we follow the perfect example of God's love, but of ourselves we can only love imperfectly at best.

We can love naturally. Parents love their children. Children, if they are treated properly and disciplined properly, usually love their parents. It happens not because the parents punish the children into loving them, but because the children have learned to trust the parents. In the love of a parent for a child, the child's very helplessness and dependence evoke feelings of love. Then the child's need and respect for parental strength and providership become the basis of love and affection. Love is simple, yet complex.

We don't love people to anything, we don't love people for anything and love has no "because" (except possibly as a response). I think the Scripture that says "We love Him because He first loved us" reflects on the fact that we love God because by loving us He showed us how to love.

I don't want people to love me for a reason. If people ever loved me because I was young, thin and good-looking, I would be utterly unloved by now. If people loved me because I was kind, I'd have a terrible time. Inhibitions about possibly speaking an unkind word would bring me to an absolute standstill.

Some Christians are like that. They walk too softly, as though the road to heaven were paved with eggs and if they broke one, they would have to turn around and go in the other direction. They mean well, but they let their doubts and fears freeze them into inaction.

That's just what the devil likes. Some say they do not believe in Satan, or at least he's not very real to them. I say that if you really tried to serve God with your whole heart, you would soon find Satan coming alongside as though he were God's helper and yours. He would not reveal the ghastly evil of his intent. He would encourage you to move forward, but at the same time speak a "word of caution" and a "word of wisdom" to slow you down and eventually paralyze you into doing nothing.

For example, if you started to think about generous church giving or tithing, along would come Satan with something like, "Yes, you certainly should give more—just as soon as you pay off some bills and set aside a few thousand dollars for your children's college fund."

Or if you thought about telling your unbelieving neighbors about Jesus and felt guilty because you had not done it yet, Satan might say, "Yes, it's terrible. They could die and go into a Christless eternity and it would be your fault. You definitely should tell your neighbors about Jesus—but remember the time you quarreled with the mailman and they saw it? Remember when you yelled at your kids and they heard? Let a little time pass until they forget. Besides, they might raise some difficult questions, so why don't you memorize 500 Bible verses and read several books on apologetics before you try to witness to them?"

Satan never tells us directly not to serve God. He merely suggests that we are inadequate and will probably fail if we move ahead. He also devises hooks that turn our good intentions into something other than what we had planned. Frequently Satan uses "buzz words" to prevent our effectiveness. We seem to like these euphemisms, and with something as important as love, you might guess we would develop many. One much-used phrase is "cheap love." I don't know exactly what that means, but surely it is not love, because there is nothing cheap about love. True love always costs something. It demands that we give ourselves, no matter what we get or do not get in return.

Another popular euphemism is "unconditional love," meaning to love someone no matter how he or she behaves toward you. We might define it as "love irrespective of the beloved's response," which is the way God loves and most parents love. It is the giving of oneself no matter how that love is received.

Other than that, love always has its conditions. Love in itself is perceived as being demanding, even though the lover makes no demands. Love makes a claim on the beloved. It invests care in the beloved. It works to the benefit of the beloved. By its very nature love is relentless. We cannot help but feel obligated to those who love us. We want to respond to their love.

Unfortunately, many do not want to accept the obligations of an appropriate response to love. Love is usually conditional because it requires attention and care. It puts conditions upon the lover. Like most euphemisms, "unconditional love" does not mean quite what we want it to mean.

In this romantic age we talk of "falling in love"—as though by mere happenstance we stumbled into this bottomless pit called love and were absolutely helpless to do anything but love. I say we can fall into lust, but not into love. We can desire to possess, because that is the true nature of lust, but the true nature of love is the desire to give, not to get. True love produces a desire to attend, not to gain the attention of another. It makes us care irrespective of whether or not our beloved cares for us.

The question then arises, "How do we love?" God gave us an imperative. Old Testament Scripture says, "Thou shalt love the Lord thy God with all thy heart, with all thy soul, and with all thy might." The New Testament says, "Love one another." If God commands us to do something, it certainly must be possible to do it through exercising the will.

But the questions remain: how do we do the thing called "love," and how do we learn to do it? As already mentioned, God provided the example of real love by giving Himself in the person of Jesus Christ to be our Savior. To love is to give. To love is to make oneself vulnerable. To love is to endure pain for another. To love is to yield up safety and security and to endure hardship to express it.

We learn to love by taking risks. We extend ourselves to people who might not love us. We give to those who may never give back. We extend care and concern where there seems no possibility of reciprocation. We reach out and make ourselves vulnerable. We endure. We take pain upon ourselves and keep on reaching.

People talk about a loving witness in evangelism. That's good. I believe that we should extend friendship and affection at the same time we extend the gospel message. But stop and think. Just giving another person the gospel—with or without friendship and affection—is the most loving thing we can do! That is love in action because it involves taking a risk. It puts our personal acceptance in jeopardy for the better good of someone's spiritual welfare.

Next to what God did in giving His only Son, giving out the gospel regardless of what the hearer may think of us is the most loving thing I know how to do! It is not easy, but it is the backbone of our Jews for Jesus ministry. It's almost time for another Jews for Jesus Summer Witnessing Campaign. For us that is a major exercise in doing the most loving—and often the most difficult—thing. We set aside personal comfort and dignity and go out on the streets to distribute gospel literature. It makes us totally vulnerable to hostile remarks and rejection—and even shoving and spitting—as we try to extend the news of God's supreme love to the spiritually needy who work and live in New York City. In the days ahead our staff and volunteer workers who will be involved in this extensive outreach will need your support and prayers more than ever!

The Comfortable Cross

The crowded room buzzed with the voices of concerned citizens. Emotions were running high at the official hearing of the Department of Parks and Recreation. The conflict revolved around a 32-foot-high lighted concrete cross on top of one of San Francisco's many hills. The cross had first been lit in 1932 by remote control from Washington, DC, by President Franklin Delano Roosevelt. For decades it had been a beacon for wayfaring seamen. Now the American Civil Liberties Union and Americans United were protesting its existence on city-owned land, and they were threatening a lawsuit to have it removed.

Christians, who valued the cross as a religious symbol for themselves and many other San Franciscans, wanted it to remain. Some secular-minded traditionalists also agreed that the cross should stay on the hilltop because it was an integral part of the city's history. Others, however, for various reasons seemed to feel threatened by this Christian symbol and lobbied vociferously for its removal.

One man sputtered angrily, "That cross is right behind my house. Every time I look out of my window I see it, and it turns my stomach. It represents a religion other than my own, and it makes me feel like I don't belong. I'm an American. I pay taxes, and I don't want to support someone else's religious symbol." The impact of his words lay not so much in what he said, but in the vehemence with which he said it.

Someone else retorted that if they removed the cross because it represented one specific group, the same logic would dictate that they also tear down the Japanese Tea Garden from the city's Golden Gate Park and stop the annual lighting of both the Christmas tree and the Hanukkah menorah in the downtown business area.

After a heated discussion, they decided that the cross could remain because it was a respected landmark as well as a Christian symbol. If the lights were to be used, their maintenance would be paid for by donations from various groups, most of them local churches. At least for the time being, the civic dispute about the cross had been resolved.

The problem of the real cross, however, is not so readily resolved. The cross of Christ remains a source of irritation to many who do not believe in Jesus and do not want to be reminded of Him. Moreover, unbelievers are not the only ones who avoid thinking about the cross and its grim significance. At times even we who believe in Y'shua and rejoice at the redemption wrought at Calvary fail to regard the cross as Scripture indicates we ought.

We like to think that we honor the cross. We sing about "the old, rugged cross." We use the symbol as jewelry and decorate our churches with it. We even preach sermons about Christ dying on the cross. Yet we seldom give serious thought to its real significance. At least we don't act as though we do.

If we did regard the cross as seriously as we should, we would attach much more importance to Y'shua's admonitions. He said, "Come, take up the cross, and follow Me" (Mark 10:21), and "He who does not take his cross and follow after Me is not worthy of Me" (Matthew 10:38).

In Greek the word Y'shua used for "worthy" is *axios*. It bears the connotation of deserving. We usually do not think very much about being worthy, but we do think a great deal about what we deserve. We tend to assume that we always deserve as much good as we can get, but we seldom think that we deserve retribution for our wrongful attitudes or actions.

Worthiness is rarely discussed these days in or out of church, but in one way or another it is a continuing problem for most of us. The working man thinks that he is worthy of as high a wage as he can get; the employer, on the other hand, feels that the working man is worth as little as he will accept. Teachers feel that their students deserve to be graded on the quality of their work, while the students usually feel that they ought to be graded on a curve based on what others have or have not accomplished.

The Bible simply says, "The laborer is worthy [*axios*] of his wages" (Luke 10:7). In other words, a worker deserves compensation for his or her labor.

Of course, in the context of salvation worthiness is another matter. Scripture states, "The wages of sin *is* death" (Romans 6:23). We are all sinners in God's sight, who without the righteousness of Christ would find ourselves eternally separated from Him. We deserve judgment because we have earned it. Not one of us can deserve the gift of salvation. The merit that allows us into God's presence is Christ's worthiness, never our own. Yet according to Y'shua's own words, the only way we can follow Him (walk with Him) is to take up our cross—die to self. When we allow our old life and our old nature to be crucified with Christ, His new life in us takes over and enables us to have fellowship with Him.

Though believers love to talk about God's great love and Y'shua's death on the cross for our salvation, none of us really wants to join Him on that cross. We want God's gift of forgiveness and grace. Yet we cling to many of our old attitudes and ways and keep our old, sinful selves very much alive.

In doing this we excuse ourselves as though God will grade our "eternal report cards" on a curve. That's a mistake. God grades all according to the standard of Jesus. In our own righteousness we simply cannot make it. All of us have flunked Righteousness 101 in the School of Life. The only way to make the grade is to die to self, and gain new life through the New Birth. Then the Holy Spirit provides us with the power to follow Him.

We know that even Paul struggled with the old self. To the church at Rome he wrote, "I find then a law, that evil is present with me, the one who wills to do good" (Romans 7:21). But Paul found the victory as he took up his cross in obedience to Matthew 10:38. To the Galatians he wrote, "I have been crucified with Christ; it is no longer I who live, but Christ lives in me; and the *life* which I now live in the flesh I live by faith in the Son of God, who loved me and gave Himself for me" (Galatians 2:20).

As I contemplated this predicament of the cross and how we usually respond to it, I spun a silly daydream. It was about a cross merchant—maybe even a cross boutique in some fashionable shopping mall. I envisioned a sign over the door: *Moe's Emporium for New and Improved Crosses.*

As you walk in, you meet the owner himself, Moe. He is smiling and well dressed. Your favorite music is being played to make you comfortable. Moe offers you a cup of coffee or a cold drink as he explains the features of the new, improved models of the cross he is selling. They are not made out of wood anymore—not only for the sake of improved ecology, but because a wooden cross is scratchy. You could get splinters from it.

Instead, the new crosses are custom-made for each wearer out of flexible plastic. In fact, they are so flexible that you can alter their shape. If you prefer, you can twist your cross to look like a crescent and star which would allow you to be fashionable around Muslims. Or when you are around Jewish people, by folding and bending you can make your cross become a Star of David so you can fit right in with the crowd.

To ensure that your cross will always stay shiny, it is coated with lacquer. And best of all, you don't have to carry your cross. It carries you. You can sit on it using a pillow or a saddle, and it is motorized to take you wherever you want to go. Should you become drowsy, your new improved cross becomes a pallet or a hammock on which you can rest. And the newest deluxe model even has a food compartment so that you can have a picnic along the way.

"So," says Moe, as he winds up his sales pitch, "if you must carry a cross and be worthy, get one of the new and improved ones that can carry you."

A far-fetched, crazy fantasy, you say? Of course. Yet don't most of us believers behave at one time or another as though we had found that new, improved, comfortable version of the cross?

There is no such thing as a comfortable cross. The cross not only represents redemption. It is a symbol of the ultimate realities of life and death. Reality is harsh. Sin is harsh, and the punishment for our sin that nailed Y'shua to the cross was harsh.

If we are to obey Y'shua's words, we must settle for that harsh, secondhand cross. It is still as heavy as sin and troublesome to carry. Yet it is worthwhile because it is Jesus' cross, and though it is far from comfortable, it is the only thing that makes us worthy before God.

As uncomfortable as that cross may be, when we take it up and die to sin and self, we find ourselves more alive than ever in Y'shua. And we have the assurance that we will continue to live with Him throughout all eternity.

CORPSES DO NOT DANCE. BRING THE LOUDEST AND BEST ORCHESTRA TO A CEMETARY, ANNOUNCE A BALL, AND INVITE THE DEAD TO JOIN IN AND DANCE. WILL THEY RESPOND AND COME TO THE GALA AFFAIR ARRANGED FOR THEM?

Unholy Tolerance

One of the most frustrating conversations I ever had was with a man whose name you would recognize because he is a high-profile evangelical leader. At a missions conference we both attended he told me, "There are people following their religions who are absolutely sincere because they are loyal to their own people, but they are not ready to hear the gospel."

The discussion was whether or not "good people" are lost. I argued back that *Jesus Christ was the only way of salvation*. Then the evangelical leader ended our conversation with, "I cannot believe that a loving God would not plan some way of salvation for those people."

I am writing about this because I feel the need to sound an alarm for God's people. There is a substantial misunderstanding today regarding the nature of salvation because there is a substantial misunderstanding about human nature. Humans do not naturally love God. They do not naturally seek Him. It is not normal for people to be saved. It is certainly not ordinary for individuals to love the Lord with all their hearts, all their souls and all their minds as Scripture commands.

Corpses do not dance. Bring the loudest and best orchestra to a cemetery, announce a ball and invite the dead to join in and dance. Will they respond and come to the gala affair arranged for them?

While that scenario is ridiculous, it has its parallel in reality. In the spiritual sense we all are stillborn. We have no viable lives. The natural person is dead in trespasses and sins and cannot respond to God's invitation. By the very substance of our humanity we are ungodly and sinful, and any religion that we might author would be corrupt and corrupting.

True Christians do not have a religion in the sense of other creeds that are authorized by human beings. We follow a revelation from God: the recorded Word of God (the Scriptures) and the Incarnate Word of God (the Savior).

Our "religion" is a response to the Holy Spirit who moves about and touches hearts, preparing people to be raised from their dead existence to new life in Christ. Our salvation is not merely a growth process. It is a creative process whereby the power of God makes alive that which was dead. That is why Scripture uses the metaphor of the new birth and we speak of being born again.

Colin Chapman, a professor at Trinity College in Bristol, England, categorizes Christians into two groups: inclusivists and exclusivists. Those who believe that non-Christians can be included to receive salvation by grace are "inclusivists." Others who, like me, believe that non-Christians have no salvation—no matter how sincere they might be—are considered "exclusivists."[1]

The problem with this kind of categorizing is that our goodwill or perspectives of people do not include or exclude them from salvation. Individuals are included or excluded on the basis of how God regards them, and the Bible states that there is no other name given under heaven or earth whereby we must be saved except the name of Jesus. Neither we nor our opinions dispense salvation. God provides salvation, and He includes or excludes whom He will.

To avoid the responsibility of obeying God, some use the common device, "It's not that simple," or to quote from one of the great American musicals, "It ain't necessarily so." I say that if God said it, it *is* necessarily so.

The Bible does contain a number of discomforting truths, such as the statement that only those who confess Christ are saved (Romans 10:9–10). Conversely, those who do *not* are *not* saved. For the sake of my parents, my ancestors, and the millions of others who have gone into eternity without Christ, I wish there were another truth. But the Scripture statements on how a person is to be saved allow for no compromise.

The biblical religion presents itself in dichotomies or statements which are diametrically opposed. There are right and wrong, purity and impurity, godliness and ungodliness, obedience and disobedience, truth and falsity, salvation and perdition. These categories are in direct opposition to one another.

In an attempt to move toward moral and ethical relativism, the world wants a big gray area between the true and the false, the good and the bad. Today's society generally chooses this approach over the biblical morality which says that good and evil are diametrically opposed to one another. One cult even maintains that Satan will be redeemed.

The civil "religion" of America is tolerance. Yet any group which presents the gospel as "the truth, the whole truth and nothing but the truth" will be rejected out of hand for its intolerance. Christians who claim, as the Bible teaches, that Christ is the only way of salvation will be labeled intolerant, because if they do not acknowledge "other ways of salvation" they are mistakenly seen as withholding equal respect and status from those who disagree with them.

Christian belief definitely has room for paradox, but there is no room to question away God's categorical statements. Those who explain away God's statements do violence to His Word.

There is such a thing as an unholy tolerance. Speaking to the situation of pluralism in his book *No Offense: Civil Religion and Protestant Taste*[2] John Murray Cuddihy wrote, "Self-definitions predicated on being 'the one true church' or 'the chosen people' are experienced in America as an unseemly ostentation, as vulgar boasting, puffing, as ridiculous even. Good taste, like St. Paul's 'charity,' flaunteth not itself, is not puffed up, does not behave itself unseemly, seeketh not her own."

Dr. Cuddihy says that those who assert a truth disbelieved by others are considered arrogant. If so, it would be considered socially unacceptable to believe *anything* very strongly—particularly if one wanted to tell others about it and possibly persuade them also to believe it.

Our modern society confuses good taste with true faith. It is considered bad taste to imply that someone might be wrong while declaring oneself to be right. That, however, is not what Christians do when they maintain that Christ is the only way to salvation. When we proclaim Christ as the only Way, we do not declare ourselves to be right. We declare Jesus to be right and ourselves to be sinners in need of rescue.

Because of an overused and much abused sense of fair play and open-mindedness, some are speaking into the evangelical church with statements on salvation so clever, sincere and kindly—yet so false—that I wonder if this is not what the Scripture means when it talks about the "doctrine of demons." The statements have been uttered in missions conferences, from pulpits and put into print. They deal with who is to be saved and how.

The doctrine is never taught; it is only implied. Clearly stated, the proposition is that a person does not necessarily need to believe in and confess Christ on this earth in order to be saved.

I heard that implication in a lecture on the uniqueness of Christ. The well-respected Christian speaker emphasized how difficult it was for religious Hindus, Buddhists and Muslims to consider Christ and concluded with, "I think we must leave it up to God to judge."

When I heard that, my somewhat sarcastic inner response was, "How kind of you to allow the Judge of the universe to be what He always has been." Because according to John 3:18, He has already judged: "He who believes in Him is not condemned; but he who does not believe is condemned already, because he has not believed in the name of the only begotten Son of God." Many evangelical leaders are reluctant to say that all religions other than what is revealed by God in Scripture are merely human opinion. Many insinuate that somehow those other religions have some validity.

I say that if kindness to our fellow human beings means that we must assign God's revelation to the status of just another human opinion, we must eschew that brand of kindness. We don't have the right to adopt the all-too-convenient device of attributing valid faith to those on whom we would bestow kindness. There is some good in other religions, but they are not salvific. To imply that they are destroys the true Christian faith.

Even to hint that there is some way of salvation other than Christ trivializes the Passion of our Savior. It renders His suffering and atoning death meaningless. Furthermore, it reduces the entire missionary movement to no more than an exercise in futility.

This Easter season is a good time to remember that no leader of any world religion, however noble, ever rose bodily from the dead—except Jesus! By His resurrection Jesus validated God's revelation. By His resurrection He showed all other religions to be less than true. As recipients of His truth, we must warn those who are deluded into thinking they are safe when, in fact, they are perishing. *How can we find the courage to say that in a loving way?*

1. Colin Chapman, "The Challenge of Other Religions," *World Evangelization*, Jan. 1989.

2. John Murray Cuddihy, *No Offense: Civil Religion and Protestant Taste* (New York: The Seabury Press, 1978).

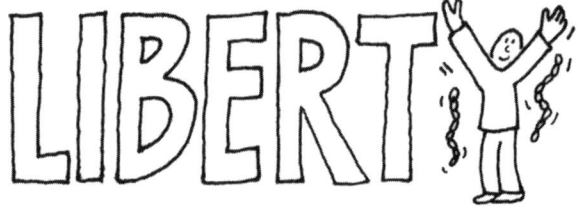

Liberty and Law

Our calendar tells us that this is the season to celebrate Independence Day. Even if we are not history buffs, many of us remember the Preamble to the Constitution, or at least the words "life, liberty and the pursuit of happiness." Our founding fathers purposed to establish or maintain a certain order and condition of existence, but the Constitution protects only life and liberty. It does not promise happiness. As for that condition of existence, we are merely guaranteed the freedom to pursue it. The Constitution gives no hint of how to obtain happiness and no reassurance that we will ever catch what we are pursuing.

There is much discussion about liberty these days. Aside from pure unselfish love, it is one of the most difficult concepts for us to understand! Many people seem to think liberty is the right to do whatever they want whenever they please, in whatever manner they choose. As our society becomes more self-indulgent, we find that we do not really want liberty but license. Whereas liberty refers only to freedom of choice, license confers the *right* to indulge or participate in some specific action. Furthermore, human nature being what it is, license can quickly deteriorate to licentiousness, which is unrestrained self-indulgence.

God's way is liberty, not license. His liberty confers on us the freedom to choose whether or not we will belong to Him and whether or not we will serve Him. When we do not commit ourselves to Him, do not serve Him and do not follow Him, then no matter which way we go, no matter whom we serve, no matter what we believe, we are *not right*.

God never forces anyone to do right. He asks us to make the right choices and gives us the liberty to decide one way or the other. If not, Joshua could not have told the Israelites, "Choose for yourselves this day whom you will serve, whether the gods which your fathers served that *were* on the other side of the River, or the gods of the Amorites, in whose land you dwell. But as for me and my house, we will serve the Lord" (Joshua 24:15).

Perhaps God allows us freedom of choice because He desires

that we love Him. Without the liberty to choose, love is impossible. Nevertheless, some people confuse liberty with independence and license.

God's world is orderly. His Law entails physical laws of nature and moral and spiritual principles that tell us how we ought to relate to Him, to our fellow humans and to the world around us. These are to be etched into our hearts and consciences by the Holy Spirit as we give ourselves to God in Y'shua.

There are also those special laws God gave through Moses to Israel. Like our national laws, God's laws were and are for the purpose of establishing and maintaining an appropriate condition of existence—in this case a life of holiness in His people, that they might be set apart in order to please Him.

God's Law cannot create holiness any more than the Constitution of the United States can guarantee happiness. God's Law can only help an individual maintain such holiness as already exists. God's Law enables the "pursuit" of the holy life, but it does not guarantee it.

In order to pursue a holy life, the believer must be redeemed, rescued and reclaimed from sin by the blood of Christ. Paradoxically, the one who is thus freed from the penalty and power of sin is to all intents and purposes a corpse, because the Scriptures tell us that sin is "toxic" even from birth and kills the soul. Therefore, before one can submit to God's Law and live a life of holiness, one more thing must be accomplished—regeneration or the new birth.

Through the new birth the redirected people of God now have the Law written in their inward parts (Jeremiah 31:33), and when they are free from sin through confession, their impulses are holy. If they follow the new impulses they will do the right thing, not because it is required or because they are compelled, but because it is now part of their nature.

In 1932, Franklin Delano Roosevelt named his social platform "The New Deal." A later president, Lyndon Baines Johnson, called his political platform "The Fair Deal." For redeemed Israel, Sinai was both a new deal and a fair deal. It did not begin with a declaration of independence, as did the United States. Instead, it began with Israel's declaration of *dependence* as they promised their obedience to God and interdependence on one another as the people of God.

The purpose of Sinai's Law was to provide for orderly relationships between God and His people, between fellow Israelites and between family members. It established property rights, propounded a fair society, promoted the worship of the Lord, made propitiation for sin, ameliorated punishment, and promised a greater rule of God yet to come—that of King Messiah. The Law prescribed worship of the Almighty but left room for innovation. It ordered stated sacrifices but encouraged spontaneity in prayer and offerings. It provided a baseline for behavior and boundaries for morality.

The Law could only be effective in "the Land" with the full consent and participation of the Israelites. There seemed no apparent penalty for failure concerning some of God's admonishments. Yet concerning social justice, God warned that He Himself would oppress those who oppressed the fatherless and widows. For the ultimate justice, penalty or reward, the final word was with the Almighty. He was to be Israel's king and Israel's judge.

The rabbis often have compared the Law to a fence. For safety, they instituted other laws, other fences, that would prevent anyone from getting too close to that original fence. Soon those fences became a prison instead of a protection. And yet, almost from the beginning, Jewish jurisprudence sought to make exceptions in order to avoid some of the obligations required by the Law. It became a "push/pull" situation. Some rabbis pushed for the enactment of more laws to keep the people from breaking the original laws, while other rabbis pulled back and rendered judgments to nullify the consequences of breaking the laws they deemed excessive or oppressive.

What had begun as a simple, straightforward set of ordinances given by God became a complex burden. If people had experienced difficulty knowing and following the Law before, by the time the rabbis had finished there was real trouble. One rabbi's *mitzvah* (act of obedience to God's commandment) became another rabbi's declaration of sinful disobedience. Confusion reigned, and even before the time of Jesus, Jewish society had become fragmented over the rabbis' pronouncements and apparent contradictions over God's Law.

Because of those problems, some see Y'shua as having come to do away with the Law. The fact is that He did not. He said, "Do not think that I came to destroy the Law or the Prophets. I did not come to destroy but to fulfill. For assuredly, I say to you, till heaven and earth pass away, one jot or one tittle will by no means pass from the law till all is fulfilled. Whoever therefore breaks one of the least of these commandments, and teaches men so, shall be called least in the kingdom of heaven; but whoever does and teaches *them,* he shall be called great in the kingdom of heaven" (Matthew 5:17–19).

Jesus came to earth not merely to deal with the Law, but to deal with the inadequacy of the human heart. Nothing about God's Law needed changing. The human heart needed changing. By His life, atoning death and resurrection, Y'shua enabled that possibility of changed human hearts through the new birth. People who have not committed their lives to God seek independence on all levels, whether governmental or in private life. National independence is not bad, but there is a kind of dependence that is better. It involves the life of faith which requires dependence upon God, and that's not so bad.

The New Covenant is God's "New Deal." It is not a new law but the new and *only* way of relating successfully to God's Law. We no longer approach God's Law as a fence or hedge that restricts our freedom. God's Law written upon the human heart by virtue of the new birth contains life. Under the New Covenant comes a new nature, a new instinct, a holy impulse and a wholeness of soul.

We need not doubt or wonder. We really know what it's all about. It's about true obedience and the opportunity to please God.

Jesus is the Man of the Law. As we are in Him and He is in us, concerning God's Law we are as complete, as whole and as healthy as He is. Y'shua is our sacrifice and our priest. He is our rabbi (teacher) and our teaching. He is the Word in which all other words find meaning. He is our king and our armor. He is our prophet and the one who enables us to heed the prophecy. He is our root and we are His blossoms. He is the vine and we are His branches. He is our judge, but He is also our advocate. In Him we stand acquitted of all wrongdoing. He is not only our lawyer but our law. As we obey Him and His teachings, we will produce the fruit of the Spirit against which there is no law (Galatians 5:22–23).

The Trouble You Need

I have a New Year's greeting for all my friends—one I know they will not receive from anyone else: In this coming year may you have as much joy, prosperity and happiness as you can contain, and may you have only enough trouble to produce in you the quality of life God desires.

That may sound like a curse instead of a blessing, but it's not. I want this to be the best year you have ever had, but my greeting stems from the recognition of what it takes to make a truly good life. Others who do not recognize that truth would wish you a year totally devoid of even one sorrowful moment, or that you would never experience anything that might cause you alarm. My prayer for you is different.

I am trying to bless you according to the biblical understanding of life. The Bible teaches that our present life, out of necessity, must include some trouble and sorrow. That's right—*trouble is necessary*! It is essential for the development of character. To ignore that fact leaves us unprepared and ill-equipped to confront the real world. That real world contains more pain than pleasure, more sickness than health and more poverty than prosperity. Only the childishly minded can hope to avoid the soul-racking pain of normal, everyday reality, but beyond this *regular reality* lies a greater reality. I call it *redemptive reality*.

In order to recognize that redemptive reality, we must lift our vision above the earthly horizon to the heavenly horizon. Redemptive reality does not minimize the fact of painful human existence. *Redemptive reality gives meaning to the pain we suffer.*

Think of the words of Y'shua to His followers: "In the world you will have tribulation [troubles]: but be of good cheer; I have overcome the world." Surely the disciples must have been confounded by the fact that although Jesus was perfection personified, earthly existence for them—and for Him—seemed as bad as ever. The ameliorating aspect of Y'shua's statement—the balm for that painful prediction—lies in that last phrase: "be of good cheer; I have overcome the world." If He is in us and we are in Him, we can be optimistic. We can even be cheerful. Though we are undergoing the pain of a present battle, Y'shua has already won the war! In Him we are eventually and ultimately winners. In Him we cannot lose, although we may suffer setbacks and incur casualties. So why worry over a war that we have already won?

We worry and fret because no one likes pain; yet pain seems to be the way of this life. But what if there were no pain? That would be dangerous. We see this in the physical realm. Some illnesses do not cause pain. They actually keep a person from feeling pain, and that is what makes them so dangerous. Hansen's Disease, better known as leprosy, is one of those illnesses. Most of us have a mental image of a leper. The victim has stumpy, fingerless hands and hobbles about on feet with missing toes or, even more grotesque, has a face without a nose. But leprosy itself does not cause those terrible disfigurements. Leprosy damages the nervous system, depriving a person of the sensation of pain. Lepers lose fingers, toes and noses because they feel no pain in those extremities when they are damaged by fire, infection or fracture. They do not react to dangers that can destroy tissue. Physical pain is a God-given warning to prevent such damage.

In much the same way, the pain and suffering of this life can work for our good. Life's sorrows can produce the resolve and repentance that enable us to turn from the soul-deadening effects of living in our godless society. The pain of sorrow is often the warning signal that redemptive reality beckons. It calls upon us to transcend our surface existence, to rise above our present circumstances and to set our hearts on that which is above.

Conversely, happy events can work as an anesthetic. They can serve to fix us in our present circumstances to the point where we lack motivation to seek the higher life. Too many believers are complacent when things are going well. They become satisfied with what they have and what they can get out of this world—until some tragedy strikes. Then the pain reminds them of the transitory nature of this temporal life.

The spiritually-minded believer knows that this life is only the process that will bring us to our eternal destiny. If we know that we are here temporarily for the purpose of accomplishing God's will, we can be comforted by life's pain rather than confounded by it. We are in a transitory state that ultimately will lead us to perfection. That process is outlined in Romans 5, which tells us that we ought to rejoice ("glory") in troubles.

At the outset that certainly sounds illogical. Trouble causes despair. To rejoice in trouble seems a direct reversal of what appears to be an appropriate and acceptable reaction. But Paul goes on to explain that we glory in troubles because they produce patience. Then patience enables us to endure, so we can perceive the true meaning of life and experience redemptive reality. The knowledge of redemptive reality gives us reason to hope, so that the adverse events of this life will not devastate us. Even in adversity we perceive and receive the love of God through Christ. Trouble produces perseverance, perseverance produces character, and the strengthening of our character enables us to grasp hope and utilize it to see into eternity itself. That knowledge of eternity with God brings security. His love fills our hearts, and we experience joy unspeakable and full of glory.

Pain is part of God's perfecting process. Its purpose is not to defeat us, but to enable us to move forward. Trouble's darkness that envelops like fog does not come to bewilder, but to enable us to see the beacon of God's love. It functions as a directional beam that enables us to move ahead in safety. The darkness of sorrow makes the yielded believer bright—a contrasting ray of God's redemptive reality.

None of us knows what troubles we will encounter next week, next month or during the coming year. It's a good thing that we do not. If we were seers and had absolute knowledge of impending sorrows and the troublous events that lay ahead, we might live with such a sense of dread that we would not see that joys also awaited us. The certain knowledge of both the pain and the good would probably prevent us from enjoying the good.

God has promised that He will not allow any trial or temptation that is beyond our ability to endure, but will provide the means for us to bear the trial, to pass the test, whatever it may be (1 Corinthians 10:13). God allows us to encounter troubles to make us strong. He is not trying to make us victims of our own sin, or victims of the sinful world around us. It is the victimization of Y'shua at Calvary that enables us who believe to be victors—now in this present life and for all eternity.

As we encounter troubles, it is enough to know that those trials serve the purpose of perfecting or completing our characters, enabling us to live in the realm of redemptive reality. Every knock can be the impetus or impulse for a boost upward or a plunge into despair. It depends on whether we are headed up or down. If our gaze is upward, toward God, He will propel us upward through every circumstance.

So then, rather than a trouble-free existence in the New Year, I wish for my friends something more: the grinding, the polishing, the perfecting and the upward propelling of our heavenly Father. May you receive from His caring hand all that you need to make you more beautiful in His sight and to cause you to shine as the stars of heaven, a beacon of God's love and grace to those around you.

Church Giving vs Missionary Giving

The time of year has come when we begin to be inundated with appeal letters from Christian and not-so-Christian organizations, all dramatizing their needs. This can become a bewildering and even disillusioning experience for those who really want to serve God and support His work. It might help you gain a proper perspective if you could regard those approaches the same way that you regard all advertising or sales brochures.

Once you carefully decide to buy a certain car, you don't worry about whether or not you should also buy two other makes and models. If you're happy with your brand of toothpaste, you don't get annoyed or anxious when you see other brands being touted over the one you regularly use. You don't become dissatisfied with your own home simply because new houses are being advertised. Nevertheless, some gracious, loving Christians react in that very manner to money appeals. They feel anxious, even guilty, because they cannot support every ministry that approaches them. Worse yet, some tender-hearted Christians divert their giving from their own churches and legitimate ministries in order to send funds to the organization that tells the saddest story, boasts of the most dramatic results, or otherwise uses manipulative techniques.

As the leader of a mission wholly dependent on God to move through His people to provide the support of Jews for Jesus, I feel that I must once again say what I've said before: As a Christian, you are obligated to support your own church or home congregation first and above all.

Pastors cannot say this. One reason they can't is that they are caught in a dilemma. They want to encourage their people to give in support of missions and Christian works; on the other hand, they know that the least worthy organizations are often the ones that do the most clamoring to promote themselves.

I am not saying that you should support *only* your local church and its ministries. God has led the most dedicated Christians to support His ministries outside of and in addition to what can be done by the local church. Nevertheless, spiritually sensitive Christians realize that their local congregation that ministers to them should have prime consideration in their giving.

I get disgusted when I hear an otherwise good Christian radio program that closes with the appeal, "Send your tithes and offerings to _____." I say to myself, "Offerings, yes, or at least maybe; tithes, no!" Tithing, or giving ten percent of one's income, is a good beginning standard. Praise God! Most Christians are able to give more than just ten percent, and a good number do. But if a person is *only* tithing, his own church should have primary consideration. You wouldn't think much of a wage earner who gave to every needy person he met on the street to the point where his own family had no food on the table for lack of funds. Yet that's exactly what many Christians do in their giving.

Five years ago when I first mentioned that concept in this newsletter, many were shocked. I guess somehow they thought that I, the leader of a faith mission, should be saying, "Support our mission first." I don't know that anyone supported our ministry less for my telling them that their first concern in Christian giving should be their local church. Since that time, however, I have received numerous letters asking about giving, tithing, etc.

One man, an old-age pensioner, wrote in anguish that he loved his church and had been a tither until his forced retirement. Because of a catastrophic illness, he had lost his home and savings. His pension was so low that he was living in one room and staying alive by eating canned dog food. He was anxiety-ridden over not being able to tithe. Belonging to a church that regularly scheduled sermons on "stewardship," he understood his pastor to be preaching from Malachi 3:8 that non-tithers were robbing God—a passage, incidentally, meant for the people of Israel living in the land. That poor man was tortured with guilt, never questioning the presumption that if a Christian did *not* give ten percent of his income, he was guilty of feloniously witholding God's due. He expressed deep shame and despair, saying, "I want to believe that God would provide if only I would trust Him by tithing. Sometimes I wonder if I have enough faith even to be saved." That man was a victim of some over-zealous preaching on stewardship. I told him that his assurance of salvation should be based on Christ, not on his ability to give—that he was saved by what God had given *him*, not by what *he* gave God!

I do believe in proportionate giving, and I think that ten percent of one's income is a good starting place. Furthermore, I won't quibble about whether the tithe should be from gross income or net income. That question removes the subject from the realm of the true nature of Christian giving. In conjunction with that, my next statement may be even more shocking: If you feel that you cannot give or do not care to give to support your local church or any Christian cause, then you should not give!

You see, only you can take upon yourself that obligation of giving to God. Theologically speaking, you could be saved if you never gave one donation to your own church or any other Christian cause. God does not love you more because you give a great deal or less because you give less. The basis of Christian giving is not giving according to some obligation, but giving out of love for God. The clearest teaching on giving is found in 2 Corinthians 9:7: "*So let* each one *give* as he purposes in his heart, not grudgingly or of necessity; for God loves a cheerful giver." What you give or do not give is a matter of what is in your heart. God loves us all anyway, but He has a special affection for those who cheerfully want to do without things because they love Him.

A while back, another friend of our ministry wrote that he was giving us substantial support because he belonged to a church that did not believe in bringing the gospel to the Jews, or at least didn't want to support any Jewish mission. I didn't tell that person what he might have done well to consider: namely, if he had strong convictions concerning mission causes that his church either opposed or was unwilling to support, perhaps he ought to look for another church. If you cannot wholeheartedly give the major part of your donations to support your own local church and its projects, you ought to think seriously about changing churches.

Of course you won't find a perfect church in your neighborhood—or in this world. And if you ever did, it would no longer be perfect after you joined it because we are all imperfect people here on earth, striving to grow toward the perfection we will achieve only in the heavenly presence of our Savior. Meanwhile, you need to belong to a church and you should support it in proportion to your income and resources. For the good of your own soul, you need to be a giver more than your church or any Christian organization needs to be the recipient of your donations. If you don't know that church membership includes an obligation to support the ministry of that church, you are indeed a rather shallow Christian. Then perhaps you ought to review first of all, your commitment to the Lord, and second, your commitment to your church.

I do hope that you will be able to continue to support your local church first, or to make that your priority for the first time if you have never before considered the matter. And I hope that as God prospers and leads, you will be able to uphold our Jews for Jesus ministry as well.

Whatever you do, it's important to remember that all of your giving is an act of worship and devotion to God. That's the way we receive gifts to our ministry because that's the way we believe they are given. True giving means giving up something. You could enjoy the worshipful act of being a sacrificial giver more than you could enjoy what you would be giving up. The key lies in contemplating what God has given you, what it cost Him, and how pleased He was when you accepted His gift of salvation in Christ. The more you realize what God has given and continues to give you, the more you'll enjoy the worship of giving to Him. So go ahead and enjoy—a lot!

Curiosity Or . . .

This morning I noticed a phenomenon that raised certain scientific questions in my mind. I frequently have such scientific questions. One time I wondered if plants might be made to grow faster by adding some tension to them. I thought of a device by which one could experiment with this hypothesis. It necessitated attaching strong thread to gentle steel springs and tying those springs to half of the test plants. Every couple of days the setup would have to be readjusted and measured to determine if those plants that were being pulled by the springs grew faster than those which did not receive similar encouragement.

I never carried out that experiment. I was just curious. This morning's curiosity did not involve another noble plan to increase the world's food supply by making plants grow faster. It was far more subjective.

After my shower I noticed that my hair seemed to dry faster than it used to. I had noticed this phenomenon several times of late. In considering the matter, the first explanation that occurred to me was that perhaps the Department of Water and Power had changed the chemical content of the water. Or perhaps it was the different shampoo I had used. As I shaved I pondered those things. Then as I ran a comb through my already-drying hair—*Eureka!*—I discovered the answer! It was not any of the eight or nine factors I had been considering. Instead, it was the simple fact that I had much less hair than I used to have. Since there were fewer hairs to get wet and more space between them, the individual strands would, of course, dry much faster.

The fact that I had substantially less hair than I used to have led me to another "scientific" deduction: people have less hair in their later years; therefore I must be getting older. Now that hardly seems possible because I usually feel like I am just beginning. I am blessed with a childlike wonder, and I am so curious about so many things. There are great books yet unread and wonderful places still unseen. But most of all, I realize that there is a whole world yet unwon for the Savior. I *am* getting older and I guess I will never read all those books, or see all those faraway places or meet all those potential friends. And likewise, in my remaining time on this earth, I will never get around to telling *everybody* about Jesus.

I ponder that last fact from time to time, and I find it somewhat disturbing. One night I had a dream about it, or perhaps I should say I had a nightmare. In my dream I saw a wide rank of people stretching like a ribbon to the horizon. They were mostly older people, but there were some younger ones as well. There were even some small children. All of them were marching in lockstep right off the edge of a precipice. There seemed to be an active volcano down below. I heard rumbles like thunder and saw flashes of lightning coming from there. Being the curious person I am, I tried to count how many people wide that rank was. And because it was a dream, I managed to do it. Each row had 32 people across. Without hesitation, together they took the same steps that led them all off the precipice into the smoking, flaming holocaust below.

Still curious, I counted and calculated. I cannot recall now how many I counted, but in the midst of my mental figuring, I was suddenly caught up in a sense of horror. What a tragedy! Before me lay all humanity, marching into a Christless eternity, and I was callously calculating how many, to satisfy my curiosity.

At that point in my dream I cried out, *"Lord, forgive me for being so callous!"* And immediately the scene changed. I was in another line of people, mostly single file, but occasionally two together, sometimes three. They were stepping upward, with joy radiating from their faces as they were lifted into the sunlight. Among them I saw some people I knew, some I had talked to. I became aware of a milieu about me. They were milling about, chatting. In that moment my hand was outstretched, and my index finger was pointing toward the horizon where the sun and the stream of people converged. I was shouting, "That's the way, that's the way. Go there!" And some did.

It was just a dream, but there was truth behind it. All too often a professional's approach to such matters is one of clinical curiosity rather than caring. The compilation of statistics does not necessarily give rise to concern. If we are not prayerfully sensitive, we may fail to remember that every person who departs this life without the Savior constitutes a tragedy of infinite magnitude.

I am glad it was only a dream, and I am glad that I am a curious person. My life has been much more enjoyable because of my innate curiosity. But my life must be more than enjoyable. It must be meaningful. It can only be meaningful if I am a *caring* person. It may sound simplistic, possibly even superstitious, but the real issue is not merely the here and now. Rather, the real issue is the reality of heaven and hell and the shortness of life.

Winter days are short, and February is a short month. Somehow that serves to remind me of the shortness of life. I have noticed recently that the years are not what they used to be for me. Each one seems a bit "shorter" than the one before. It makes me more aware than ever that I must use my time wisely; that I should be seeking more ways to tell more people that God cares for them enough to send His Son to die for them, and that He wants them to respond to Him.

In considering the shortness of life, some might sermonize that we ought to treat each moment as possibly our last. Others might argue with equal fervor that we ought to relax and approach life with long-range plans. I have operated at times in each mode. I don't mean to be morbid, and I have come to a conclusion: Panic is not the answer to life's brevity, and there may be more time than we fear there is. On the other hand, there may be less time than we think. In any case, there is *no* time we can afford to waste.

I am eagerly looking forward to seeing my Savior face-to-face some day and being in His physical presence forever. I would like that moment of greeting to be without regret over squandered opportunities. I would prefer to have my life's net overflowing with the souls of people. I would like it so full that my boat tips and rocks precariously as I approach that final shore. With Him to guide and secure me, it will not be a risky maneuver after all, and I long to hear Him say, "Well done!"

DISCONNECTED FROM GOD THROUGH SIN, OUR LIVES HAVE BECOME FRAGMENTED.

The Disintegrated Personality

God gave Israel the Day of Atonement as a time for soul-searching, repentance and restoring broken relationships with Him. Today many consider this concept of returning to God and seeking His acceptance archaic and irrelevant. For the most part, our twentieth-century society has not been raised to accept obligations toward others, let alone obligations toward God, who is Wholly Other.

It is neither natural nor common for people to want to be joined to God. "Why," they reason, "must we be at one with anything or anyone?" In an age that exalts individuality and identity, many find the idea of conforming almost offensive. In all seriousness, they ask, "Why shouldn't everyone have their own way, as long as they don't harm anyone else?" They ask that question as if somehow it were possible for people absolutely to have their own way without hurting others. They ask as though they deserve whatever they want and there is enough of everything for everyone to have and be the best and the most. They speak as though wanting and desire never lead to lust, and as though lust and greed never lead to aggression, and as though each component of a person's life is separate and needs nothing to make it part of the whole.

All this self-centeredness and greed do not arise from ordinary needs. They stem from a pandemic disease that afflicts every living person. That disease, spiritual heart trouble inherited from our father Adam, is what God calls "sin." From the depths of our hearts all humanity is sinful.

The metaphor of the heart refers to the innermost being. The Old Testament Hebrew *lev*, which is translated as "heart," is better translated "innards." Sometimes in the Old Testament *lev* is also rendered "bowels." It matches our modern slang word "guts," often used to indicate fortitude, courage and resolve.

Another familiar term, "together," began in the '70s with the "flower children." A "together" person was one who had emotional stability and knew what he or she wanted and where he or she was going in life. In God's sight, however, we are all "untogether." Disconnected from God through sin, our lives have become fragmented.

The goal of the whole person is to serve God, but through the "sin disconnection" the various components of the personality mushroom outward, away from the center. The emotions become monsterized. Proper concern for food and shelter turns to greed. The desire to love and give changes to lust and a desire to use and consume. Ordinary need for protection is distorted into prejudice, suspicion and mistrust. A minor annoyance becomes a major affront. An inconvenience becomes an impossible situation. This happens because all the elements of our lives are pulling against each other, creating unbearable tensions that can leave us quaking with unimaginable fear, untenable anger or unbearable desire.

When this happens, like Humpty Dumpty in his fall, we break and splatter. But unlike Humpty Dumpty, of whom it was said, "All the king's horses and all the king's men couldn't put Humpty together again," God *can* put us together again.

In sin we are not merely disheartened, we are "disemboweled," but there is a cure. We can be given new "innards." Atonement is the solution to sin and its consequences of alienation from God, self and society. Atonement, the condition of being at one, heals the disintegration of soul and spirit and repairs the broken heart.

In seeking a panacea for the human condition apart from God, we often fail to recognize that people are turned against themselves. They change direction so frequently that they never arrive at their intended destination and never reach their life's goals.

Imagine a person who has struggled hard to qualify for and complete medical school. From his earliest self-awareness he has wanted to relieve physical suffering and save lives. He has become a virtual slave to that purpose, enduring great hardships to achieve his education, working inhuman hours to complete a difficult internship and finally a residency.

He performs brilliant emergency room work, but then he

takes a slightly different direction. Seeking to develop a specialty, he decides on plastic surgery so he can help those who suffer from congenital deformities and disease-related disfigurement. As he specializes in plastic surgery, he is drawn to the most lucrative aspect of that field which involves hair transplants, face lifts, tummy tucks, liposuction—and relatively few emergencies. Certainly there is nothing wrong with a branch of medicine that serves to improve human appearance, but in this case, has that doctor not become somewhat disconnected from his original purpose of selflessly spending himself to save human lives and alleviate suffering?

Usually the disconnection of a person from his or her major goals is not so perceptible. Consider the believer who loves the Lord so much that he wants to be a minister. Since he is a dynamic person who can gather a flock and is already a gifted speaker, he feels he need not submit to any formal training. He tells himself and others that he will continue to study as he ministers, or he may even take the pietistic position that God will teach him all he needs to know. (That is not to imply that God does not teach people, or that there are not some effective ministers who have had no formal training. Yet this is not the usual way.) Finally, worst of all, it may never occur to that untrained or self-trained minister that the flock he seeks to gather deserves more from him than he is willing to give in order to be an effective pastor.

That once idealistic emergency physician who has limited himself to cosmetic surgery and that committed Christian who wants to minister without training share a common flaw. Each has become detached from his intended goal! The physician has forgotten why he first sought medical training, and his noble motivation has faded and changed. The untrained minister, in wanting to avoid the difficult process of training, also has become disconnected from his high calling and destiny.

When such major disconnections in one life become many—and this often happens—we say that the personality is disintegrating. The disintegrated personality does not lead immediately to a crumbled consciousness. Instead it leads to a changed sense of reality and a changed value system.

The primary disconnection, however, is the disconnection from God as our source of strength, direction and knowledge. That one disconnection leads to many disconnections, so that the individual becomes a disintegrated personality.

The integrated personality is connected to the purpose of being. Well-integrated individuals understand their purpose in life and are able to focus on the process of developing themselves to fulfill their destinies. Totally integrated personalities are at one with self because they are at one with God. They draw their sense of reality from the Creator and Sustainer of the universe.

The act of atonement is just what it sounds like—the joining of God and man, so that we enter into this state of at-one-ment. The potential for that condition was initiated and achieved by God at Calvary, but we must enter it by faith.

This is a very solemn time of year when Jewish people are commanded to afflict their souls in contrition for sins. Nevertheless, it can be a time of celebration as well if we know our sins are forgiven. As we approach the Day of Atonement, we who are Jews for Jesus contemplate the finished work of Christ at Calvary. We meditate and give thanks for the oneness we have with God because of His atonement for our sin. We invite all who have experienced this oneness to rejoice with us, for Y'shua has turned our mourning into joy. Christ our Savior died for our sins, and now we are integrated with God Almighty. Praise His name forever!

On the Cutting Edge

I am not a recreational shopper. Wandering from store to store is not much fun for me. Seeing too much merchandise bewilders me and makes me weary. There is one kind of store, however, that grabs my attention and gets me excited. That is a cutlery shop. I like almost everything they have, from the kitchen implements to the tiny tweezers; but I especially love the knives. I am fascinated by a good, well-sharpened knife that cuts effortlessly.

In my briefcase I carry a red Swiss Army knife. It has all kinds of blades—a screwdriver, a file and even a saw. In my pocket I carry another, smaller Swiss Army knife that has a scissor. At home I have a couple of good kitchen knives that were made in Solingen, Germany. They are high carbon steel, and each one cost me more than a day's wages when I bought them a long time ago. I don't like my wife Ceil to use them. It's not that I begrudge her the use of anything I have. Everything I have is hers, and she always takes good care of my things—but she does not take good care of herself when using a knife. Several times a year she receives a cut or nick of varying severity from using a kitchen knife. For that reason she is glad to avoid using the couple of better knives that I keep razor sharp. I do use them occasionally, and when I do, it always brings me a brief moment of supreme satisfaction.

I also own an old-fashioned straight-edged razor and leather strop like those used by our grandfathers. I shave with it occasionally. When I was a boy, just beginning to shave, my father was using the more common safety razor. But I bought that straight-edged razor and learned how to use it without wreaking havoc on my face. It takes me three minutes to prepare the razor and my face for two minutes of shaving, but every time I use that straight-edged razor I feel like a master craftsman. It really does not take much more time or effort to shave with that six-inch blade than it does to use one of the newer kinds of razors, but I must be very, very careful. That is the problem of using something sharp. One can cut what was not intended to be cut.

Once a chef told me that you cannot wear out a truly good

knife, even if you use it every hour of every day for a lifetime. That is probably an exaggeration, but I do know that the quality of a blade depends upon the quality of the steel, and that good steel requires a careful tempering process. My razor and a couple of my knives have been sharpened hundreds of times. At each sharpening some of the edge was ground away. Yet the amount lost has always been so infinitesimal that they look the same as when I first bought them.

In describing our ministry, one church leader said, "Jews for Jesus is on the cutting edge of evangelism." That was more of a compliment than he probably realized. The metaphor pleased me greatly because that is just where I would want our ministry to be—on the cutting edge of evangelism, using the sword of the Word to slash the bonds of a world alienated from the One who longs to redeem it. Furthermore, that pastor's perceptions were good. In order to make a cutting tool sharp, one must keep the edge thin, but also make sure that it is thin at the correct angle. Otherwise, the first time it is used it will lose its edge and become dull again.

I like to think that Jews for Jesus is that right kind of thin. Our ministry began with people who, like good knives, were an alloy of experience. First God's Word slashed through our preconceived notions, religiosity or philosophies and brought us to the feet of the Savior. Then, as we went out to share the Good News of Messiah with our fellow Jews, we were hard-forged in the fires of opposition. Those who know us well have sometimes observed a gentle abrasiveness in the manner we have with one another. Like steel upon steel, we keep each other sharp. Each of us, like a good knife tempered in the fire, must be sharpened constantly, and that process of sharpening involves abrasion at the correct angle.

Unlike knives, some people resist any kind of abrasion, and they become dull. If Jews for Jesus is on the cutting edge of evangelism, it is because we know that in order to be sharp, we must keep a thin front. That means we maintain a narrow focus. People keep writing to us to say how much they enjoy our television program—except we don't have a television program. Others tell us how much they enjoy our monthly magazine—except we don't print one. Obviously they are confusing us with some other ministry. But we don't have those things for a reason. We do not diversify because we want to keep a narrow focus and a sharp edge.

A few weeks ago while handing out gospel tracts in Washington, DC, I encountered a fellow Christian. He had a cheery smile and a word of encouragement for me. When he told me that he received our newsletter and enjoyed reading Moishe Rosen's articles, that became the occasion for me to introduce myself and accept his compliment. At that he seemed surprised that I would be standing on the street myself handing out tracts. Maybe he thought that Jews for Jesus was much bigger than we are and didn't need me to do that. Maybe he thought I was "too important" to do that.

At Jews for Jesus we have more than a hundred staff workers, but none of us who have ever been missionary-evangelists will ever get to the point where we are "too good" or "too important" to hand out tracts in public places. I feel that I, in particular, need to hand out tracts on the streets because I write so many of them. I need to see how people interact with the literature we are distributing.

At Jews for Jesus we can be sharp because we are operating on a narrow front. Sure, there are times when I dream about having our own film and video production centers and having our own album production studios. But the biggest dream I can allow myself for the time being is that we might get a four-color press so that we can print better tracts.

The Word of God is sharper than any two-edged sword, and distribution of tracts that proclaim that message is the cutting edge of evangelism. If we allow ourselves as a missionary organization to become too broad—too diversified—we will lose our cutting edge. Likewise, if we should try to avoid the abrasion that sharpens us, we would lose our cutting edge. The abrasion that sharpens a knife does not hurt that inanimate object. The frailty of our human flesh, however, does cause pain as we are subjected to the sharpening process. If we accept the trimming and grinding, we keep sharp; if we seek to avoid it, we grow dull and lose our effectiveness. (Many a good roast has been ruined because of a dull carving knife. The roast was hacked up and served in tasteless, stringy lumps.)

During the month of July Jews for Jesus will be on the extreme cutting edge once again as we proceed with our annual Summer Witnessing Campaign. Depending on the circumstances, we may be able to hand-deliver as many as two million of our gospel broadside tracts. We know that the schedule will be rigorous, and that the opposition can be fiery. Your prayers will serve to strengthen the steel of our resolve to make Christ known.

Enduring

It has been said that God loves the sinner but hates the sin. I love airplanes, but I hate flying. However, unlike God, who hates sin and never sins, though I hate flying, I fly a great deal. I fly because I love God and want to serve Him, and in order to do that most efficiently I often must travel. I'm not afraid of flying. It's just that the crowding is so bad and the air is so poor that sometimes crashing would seem almost a welcome relief. It would mean that all of my work on earth was finished, because I know that God will not call me home one minute before I'm done with the task He has given me.

In the meantime, for the sake of expediency I just keep on flying. I have learned that serving God often involves some measure of discomfort. It's not always physical discomfort, like sitting in a crowded plane and breathing bad air for hours at a time. Sometimes it's emotional discomfort. Nevertheless there's always a price to pay—something to endure.

Somehow many believers have the notion that if something is from God it never involves difficulty. While at times God allows us to accomplish good things with ease, that is not the norm. When God wanted to accomplish our redemption He had no easy way for His Messiah. Jesus was no masochist. He did not enjoy deprivation or suffering. Though He often lacked comfort, He knew how to accept it when it was appropriate. He didn't turn down Mary's expensive ointment. He knew how to rejoice, as when He attended the wedding at Cana. Many of His teachings contain jokes, and somehow I see Him smiling a great deal and even laughing.

But in one area Jesus differed. Whereas He could enjoy the comforts of life, the companionship of friends and gestures of affection, and whereas He had patience for children and probably enjoyed their company, He was self-wielding. He managed to endure what He had to endure. Besides the ultimate pain of Calvary, throughout His ministry on earth Jesus had to endure the misunderstanding and contempt of those who did not want to believe in Him.

How difficult it must have been for the almighty, all-seeing, eternal, all-knowing God to set upon Himself the limitations of being human—to crawl in His infancy, and to need a mother's care. How much self-control Y'shua must have exercised not to make a mighty display of His power and show those scribes and Pharisees who He really was. He could have called on twelve legions of angels (Matthew 26:53) when He was on the cross. Why didn't He? Could He not have counted Himself crucified, just as God had counted Isaac as having been offered to the benefit of Abraham? But no, Y'shua did not seek the easy way. Part of His divine nature was His ability to endure what needed to be endured.

Enduring builds character. We do not grow strong by saying "yes" to ourselves, but by saying "no" when necessary. If we avoid giving in to that which might cause us to fail, we may win that which God wants us to gain for Him. Enduring is the hardest work required by faith.

Enduring is anchored in the past, where we have taken our stand. It is practiced in the present, one step at a time. It is oriented to the future, where we have God's promise of relief from all pain and a glorious fulfillment of all human longing. Enduring is our part of what God has enabled us to do because of what He accomplished at Calvary. It is our human counterpart to the divine work of sanctification.

Sanctification is not a dour process of denying all of life's enjoyments. Rather, it is the selection and appropriation of healthy enjoyments and the rejection of all that distracts us from serving God. Holiness is anything but somber! It is a mind-expanding, consciousness-raising, soul-magnifying state of existence. The endurance which is so necessary if we would gain the best of life involves several stages. Sometimes they are simultaneous. They include **wanting, waiting, walking** and **working.**

Christians fail, not because they want to avoid doing what is right, but because they do not exercise the necessary will to stand firm where they have positioned themselves in Christ. **Wanting** is a matter of motivation. Nobody ever became holy or did the right thing unconsciously. It takes a conscious commitment to want what is right.

Motivation is difficult to marshal when we take our gaze from God. King Solomon wrote, "Where there is no revelation, the people cast off restraint" (Proverbs 29:18). When we see God, His splendid majesty, goodness and love for us, all focused through the atoning death of the Messiah at Calvary, we are moved to want what is right. Our power to be motivated to care and to want the right thing must be that vision of God's love at Calvary.

Once we are moved to want the right thing, we often find that we must **wait** on the Lord. Think of the apostles. Dynamically charged up by the presence of the risen Christ, they wanted to get on with the work of the Kingdom, but the King told them to wait at Jerusalem for the coming of the Holy Spirit. Only then would they begin the task of the Great Commission. It is axiomatic of the life of faith that when we go to God in prayer ready to do His will, He answers our prayer proposals in one of three ways. Sometimes He says "Yes" and sometimes "No." But even more often He says, "Wait!"

When God's answer is "Yes" He usually asks us to **walk** with Him. He sets off in a certain direction and promises only to show us our role bit by bit as we follow. We set off to walk with the Lord as did Abram. As we go, God usually informs us on a "need to know" basis. This usually causes chagrin to the new or untrusting believer who wants to know every detail of the task. But the experienced believer does not need to know all the particulars of what lies in store, nor how to deal with each problem or situation that will arise. All that believer needs to know is that God is there to direct whenever action is needed.

When God's work must be done, He shows us what to do and how to proceed. The Hebrew word for work is *avodah*, which means labor, but it also means worship and service. It is said that Ruth Bell Graham has a sign over the kitchen sink where she washes dishes that says: "Divine service performed here three times daily." There is a God-honoring way of washing dishes or shoveling coal or working at an assembly line by which a person can honor the Lord as much as by doing the work of an evangelist.

What makes our waiting, wanting, walking or working holy and part of our sanctification process is our decision to endure it for the glory of God. As believers, our hearts have been **wakened** and sensitized by our vision of Calvary. It's all summed up in a song I wish we all sang more often:

Turn your eyes upon Jesus.
Look full in His wonderful face
And the things of earth will grow strangely dim
In the light of His glory and grace.

God is Not a Sourpuss

Many people imagine God as some kind of cosmic faultfinder. They see Him as a stern judge who is obsessed with their every defect, and is perpetually annoyed with them because they are not as perfect as the Adam He created. To counterbalance this image of stern disapproval, Pharisees—both ancient and modern—have devised countless self-imposed rules and restrictions. Their quest for divine approval leads to pride in what they do or avoid doing, and smugness about tithing down to a sprig of mint or a bit of cumin. Not only do they take issue concerning small matters, but they also feel the need to instruct others to follow their example to the letter. Such people think that true godliness demands their services as ophthalmic surgeons and fruit inspectors. They are constantly trying to remove splinters from poor sinners' eyes and assessing the quantity and quality of the harvest in the lives of others.

The saddest thing about such Pharisees is not their self-righteousness, but their distorted notion of God. They see Him as being cold and stern—severe and grim. And they themselves become like the God of their imagination—severe and unloving.

Fortunately God is not like that at all. He is perfect in Himself, but He is not a perfectionist toward us. A. W. Tozer, twentieth-century spokesman for the Christian and Missionary Alliance Church, once said, "How good it would be if we could learn that God is easy to live with. He remembers our frame and knows that we are dust. He may sometimes chasten us, it is true, but even this he does with a smile, the proud, tender smile of a father who is bursting with pleasure over an imperfect but promising son who is coming every day to look more and more like the one whose child he is."[1]

Of course the entire concept of God as our loving Heavenly Father is predicated upon our relationship to Him. According to Scripture, God is the Creator of all, but not the Father of all. Faith in Christ makes us His children. To us who believe, God is the perfect Father—and because He is perfect, He knows that we, His children, are still growing. While often our behavior may leave much to be desired, and at times we may seem to lack progress or even suffer defeats and setbacks, He remains patient.

As the perfect Father, God looks at us who are in Christ and beholds the countenance of His perfect Son. He knows that one day in heaven we will be like Him. And because of that perfect sonship He has begun to form in us, He can be patient; He can be merciful.

Nevertheless, because He is the perfect Father, there are times when God must chasten an erring child. But even that bit of correction, grievous as it sometimes is, proves to us that we are indeed His children. I never cease to take comfort in the passage that says, "For whom the Lord loves He chastens, and scourges every son whom He receives. If you endure chastening, God deals with you as with sons; for what son is there whom a father does not chasten?" (Hebrews 12:6–7).

It is a sad parent-child relationship that is based only on fear without love. However, there is a healthy and appropriate "fear" that entails proper respect. In that sense, we ought to "fear" our earthly parents and God, our Heavenly Father. The Scriptures teach that "the fear of the Lord is the beginning of wisdom." To insure a productive relationship with our Heavenly Father, we ought to maintain a holy reverence and respect and try to please Him by doing well. Nevertheless, our relationship with the Heavenly Father *is* based on love. Thankfully, however, it is based not on *our* love for Him, but on *His* love for us—the love that sent Y'shua to the cross for our sins. Again, the Bible says it better than I ever could: "We love Him because He first loved us" (1 John 4:19).

I love God, and I hope that you do too. I love Him not just because He commands us to love Him. The command, in and of itself, would be ineffectual without the knowledge that God is loving. God is merciful; He cares for me. He knows my every weakness; He knows how often I fail him. Yet He forgives and upholds me, and He draws me closer. I love Him because I am discovering more and more that He is utterly worthy of my love.

The Pharisees of Y'shua's day, and the Pharisees of our time as well, tried and are trying so hard to be righteous that they miss the mark. Not only do they fail to please God, but they also *in*cur and *con*fer misery in the wake of their agonizing efforts. To quote A. W. Tozer once again, he summed up this kind of right gone wrong when he wrote:

> There are areas in our lives where in our effort to be right we may go wrong, so wrong as to lead to spiritual deformity. To be specific let me name a few:
>
> 1. When in our determination to be bold we become brazen.
>
> 2. When in our desire to be frank we become rude.
>
> 3. When in our effort to be watchful we become suspicious.
>
> 4. When we mean to be conscientious and become overscrupulous.[2]

"Spiritual deformity"—I can think of no better description for the Pharisees, ancient and present. I do pity the poor Pharisees of today. In their misguided zeal they tend to replace their freedom in Christ with shackles of human design. Surely they must lack joy. They "know" more rules than God ever gave, but they don't know the heart of the Giver. If they did know, they could relax instead of wringing their hearts to squeeze out a drop or two of righteousness.

---

1. A. W. Tozer, *The Root of the Righteous*
2. A. W. Tozer, *That Incredible Christian*

Of Mice and Birds

My house is built into the side of a hill. In my home I have an office. Outside my office window I can see the top of a twenty-five-foot-high eucalyptus tree. Sometimes squirrels climb that tree or hop down to it from an overhanging telephone wire, but more often the tree hosts a variety of neighborhood birds.

Very early one morning before I was ready to concentrate on some serious work, I saw a bird fly up and perch on the topmost branch of my eucalyptus tree. As I watched, a stiff ocean breeze pushed the little bird in one direction while the tree branch still swung the other way. I thought to myself, "It's a good thing that bird is not a tree-climbing field mouse. If he were, he'd fall off for sure."

Then in my imagination, in the realm of daydreams and far-fetched things, I thought of a strange scenario involving birds and mice: in its highest branches my eucalyptus tree might cradle a bird's nest of twigs and grass, while the cavity at the base of its trunk cozily housed a family of field mice.

I pictured a bird's egg falling out of that high nest. Against all odds, it would not break and would roll into the mouse hole on the ground. Discovering the egg, the mice might think it made a nice pillow. They would all huddle around it and rest their furry little heads on it while they slept—until one day the egg would begin to vibrate and make strange noises. It would crack open, and out would wiggle a baby bird. In that mouse nest there would be little mouslings—or whatever baby mice are called—and the baby bird would grow up with them. It would think that it, too, was a mouse. Mimicking its mouse siblings, it would scurry about on the ground looking for seeds and small insects to eat.

But then I thought, if that bird grew up in a mouse environment thinking it was a mouse, it would react to its natural instincts and eventually it would become restless and lonely, particularly at mating time. Then perhaps the bird that thought it was a mouse would seek adventure. It would climb up my eucalyptus tree (though I have never seen a real mouse climb to the top of the tree). Then perhaps my imaginary bird would find itself swinging in the wind like the real bird I had seen. Perhaps it would clutch at that topmost branch much the way I saw the real bird clutching it in the high wind. And perhaps the wind would blow so hard that it would actually dislodge the bird who thought it was a mouse.

Then, in its desperate attempt to keep from falling, the little creature would flap its unused front "feet" which, unknown to it, were really wings. And in that moment of high wind the mouse-minded bird would discover that it could fly—that it could soar—that it need not spend its entire life grubbing around on the ground on spindly, unsuitable legs.

As I came out of my reverie I thought, believers in Jesus are sometimes like that bird I dreamed up. Far too often we think we are mice when we are really birds. Finding ourselves in a base environment, we fail to realize that we have the God-given equipment that enables us to soar above our circumstances. We fail to realize that we need not eke out our lives on that lower plane—that we need not fear those base things that prey on ground animals, because the New Birth has made us different creatures. We fail to realize that we can remain stable when shaken, or even soar higher when necessary.

Because we forget who we are in Christ, many of us never do get off the ground. Some of us dare to investigate and climb a bit higher, but invariably we end up clinging to one of the lower branches, afraid to go too high. Sometimes it takes a very strong wind of adversity to blow us off the branch to which we are clinging. Just when we think we are falling and will surely perish, the same wind that blew us off the branch lifts us, and we begin to fly. Then we begin to get an inkling of what God really intends for us to be.

As humans we are mere "mice" who will eke out our lowly existence on the ground until we die. But in Christ, and by the power of His Spirit, we are "birds." In Christ God has transformed us into beings who can soar to spiritual heights and transcend our lowly mortal experiences. We need not be battered and buffeted by every chance wind that overtakes us. We can fly above the storms of life and bask in the warmth and sunshine of a brighter day to come.

Why am I telling you my daydream? I guess what I wanted to say was, "Let's get out of our mouse costumes and stop being content to grub around on the ground. Let's find our wings. Let's gear up to fly, because there's work to do, and because that's what our Heavenly Father has in store for us—in this life and in the life to come."

"Beloved, now we are children of God; and it has not yet been revealed what we shall be, but we know that when He is revealed, we shall be like Him, for we shall see Him as He is. And everyone who has this hope in Him purifies himself, just as He is pure" (1 John 3:2–3).

Lessons

Most of these lessons are taken from talks Moishe gave to the Jews for Jesus leadership at our quarterly Council meetings. Some are from his training lectures. Other extracts are from our newsletters.

In *Called to Controversy: The Unlikely Story of Moishe Rosen and the Founding of Jews for Jesus*, Moishe used a phrase "practical piety" to describe the outworking of his faith. You'll see much of that practical piety in these lessons.

The "you" Moishe referred to in most of these extracts was the Jews for Jesus leadership, but his lessons have a far wider application. Some themes that were key to building our staff and our ministry overlap in all three parts of this book as principles that apply to all believers. We hope they add a dimension of insight, not only to your understanding of Moishe Rosen and Jews for Jesus, but also to daily issues you are facing in your own life.

Smaller extracts—up to a few paragraphs in length—are listed in alphabetical order by topic. Longer extracts follow.

Admonitions

How many times do we need to be admonished to give, to love, to serve? We need these admonitions until we believe perfectly, give perfectly, serve perfectly and love perfectly.

***

Good workers will not hate you for letting them know they did something poorly. If you are fair about it, they will love you.

Advice Giving

Often when people ask for advice, they want something else. Sometimes they want to be affirmed in what they've already decided. Sometimes they want to be urged to action. Sometimes they don't know what they want. Rather than telling someone what is right, help him or her to discover it. Ask what their options are, ask questions that help them identify those options and pray with them to be able to take the best option, the one that will be what God would want and that will glorify Him.

Authority

The purpose of authority is to facilitate and to see that the standards and quality are maintained.

Backsliding

I've seen people "backslide," go into all manner of sin only to return to the Lord after a lengthy season. Always treat them like they can and will return. People change. God changes people.

Compassion has to be there all the time. Forgiveness has to be there all the time. Even sorrow can help us learn and grow. Defeats can turn into victories.

***

Some of you are having trouble with your spiritual lives because you think that you've arrived, and the destination does not look so good. But you don't realize you've stopped along the journey and you're still quite short of the goal.

***

There is no such thing as frontsliding. But backsliding always begins with a stop. You are moving ahead, and then you stop along the way to take a rest, because it is difficult to keep moving closer to God. You relax on that hill of life; you put on the parking brake. The car is in gear, but you don't notice that you parked in a puddle of grease. The whole hill is greasy. Your car starts sliding backwards, slowly at first and maybe you don't notice. You're just relaxing. Maybe it's even fun as you slide faster and faster. You want to say, "Whee! This is a fun roller coaster!" But there's no up: only down. The grease is always there.

***

Someone on staff had his feelings hurt when I inquired about his spiritual life. He told me in most reassuring terms that he was as close to the Lord as ever, but he never asked me why I made the inquiry. And why would I ask? Because all signs said he was skidding backwards on the grease of self-centered concerns. All the signals I could see were indicating that direction. We do signal to each other and tell our condition more than most realize. Otherwise we wouldn't be able to pray for and uphold one another.

***

It's easy to backslide in the ministry because you don't have any of the warning signs that other Christians have. You're going through all the motions of being godly. Let me tell you this: if the going seems easier, it's probably because you're headed downhill.

Balance

God wants us to be balanced people. There's a balance and a tension between personal life and professional life. You can't rob from one to give to the other. There's a balance between what you allow yourself for recreation and personal development, and what you refuse to allow yourself so that work can get done. We don't look to create tension but we need to recognize those tensions that naturally exist or we will be pulled too much in one direction or the other and be thrown off balance.

* * *

Everybody needs time off, but when your time off becomes the main subject of your discussion, what are you saying about your work? Now if we don't love our work, then we've got a real problem. I love my work so much and I hope that each of you do, too. I don't want people working under me unless they want my job. I want you to want it because it means so much to me and I know that it could mean that much to you. And you want people working under you to want your job. If they don't want your job, if they say they'd never want your job, you have failed to convey to them the joy that you have in ministry.

* * *

Whenever possible, keep eternity in your heart and mind, but balance that with the fact that your life is *not* going to begin when you get or do something you want. Your life is now, today, and the quality of your life is determined by your relationship with God moment by moment.

Bearing One Another's Burdens

Sometimes you can pull someone else's load over a rough spot they can't manage. You bring a new perspective. We often have blind spots that others can see. People can get so busy trying to solve their problems that they overlook the obvious. If everybody took the responsibility to help pull another's load, most things would get done very easily.

***

When you are bearing someone's burden, remember that roles change. I recently realized that I tend to forget I am no longer in a teacher mode with certain people. I mistakenly tend to lecture and instruct those no longer under my tutelage. It's important to listen to what the other person has to say. Make yourself available to bear the other person's burden. But remember relationships and roles change. Don't pull an old load which is no longer your burden.

Bigger Is Not Better

One of the big problems of the church in America and overseas is the idea that bigger is better, believing that somehow the more people you involve, the higher the level of dedication. It doesn't work that way, because you can't give yourself to too many people.

***

Would you be satisfied to have a Bible study of just twelve like Jesus did? You get the twelve right people, handpicked people, and you'll turn the world upside-down.

Burnout

It has become popular to use the term "burnout" to describe those who have worked themselves into a state of exhaustion and despair. I don't like the term. Think in terms of a kerosene or oil lamp. When does it burn out? When there is no more fuel. Our fuel is the Holy Spirit. Except for a few instances, I am not worried about overworking people. But there comes a time when a person is burning wick rather than fuel—the wick chars and does not produce much light. If that happens, it is best to extinguish the light until the lamp has been refueled.

Commitment and Community

We are not to command people, we are to commend them. We are to commend them to God and commend God to them. When we commend people to one another we make them part of the whole. We get them relating to one another, and this is reproductive. Do you have people who are serving the Lord and ministering for the Lord because you cared for them and committed yourself to them? The secret of being a leader is God's secret: He "commends His love toward us, in that, while we were yet sinners, Christ died for us." He committed Himself to us so that even though we might reject Him, He was still committed to us. We can learn from God.

***

Community involves commitment. It touches every aspect of one's life; where you live, how you live, who you accept as your circle of friends. When you belong to a community, you don't just say, "I'm part of the group," but you work to make yourself part of the group by where you move, by those with whom you associate, by accepting the group standards. And sometimes, these might not be your particular standards.

A commitment to God should mean a commitment to other godly people, to bear one another's burdens, to rejoice with one another, to foster one another's growth, to be submitted to one another, to have the counsel of one another. The role of the professional minister is far less important than the role of the natural elders, the lay people who put themselves out for the congregation.

***

Give a lot to a few. That's the way that you can give more. Learn to make commitments to people and to get commitments from those who will keep their commitments. Establish informally committed relationships.

***

We need to require things of others. A true godly community must maintain expectations. If we do not have expectations of one another then we will not understand the boundaries of our relationships. We depend upon one another and therefore we expect from one another. There can be no community without accountability and expectations.

***

Loving the Lord requires us to love others and include them within our faith community. Perhaps this is one of the reasons that churches do not grow. They are too picky about whom they might include and too impatient with the God who can change the unlovely into something beautiful by His power and grace. Let's face it—some of you were not so lovable when I first met you. What if I decided not to include you in what I saw God doing through our little group?

Brothers and sisters, if we are to grow as God wants us to grow then we must open up in faith to others, even if they might seem unlovable at the present time. To deny them a place in our community is to limit God who promises to transform each person who accepts Y'shua. We must be a people who readily believe 2 Corinthians 5:17—for the Lord is able to make new people out of all those who receive Him.

We are not a community of the perfected, but a community of the redeemed. One day we will be perfected, but until that day we will be far less than what He and we want. Yet as a community on the move for the Messiah, we can make a difference—if we stand together.

Common Misconceptions

Guard yourself against thinking that:

- you deserve anything you can get from people.

- if you have enough money, you can get anything done.

- the more people involved, the better.

Competition

If I've had any success in life, it's that I've refused to compete with other people. I've competed only with myself, because I'm not trying to be better than them, I'm trying to be better than me. Can I do better, can I beat myself? That's the way you have to think. It's not just when things go wrong but when they go right as well that we should ask, "What could I have done better?" When you find an area where you're gifted and you do very well in something, that's where you really concentrate on doing better because you can excel.

***

You aren't a winner because someone else is a loser. You are a winner because you help other people grow and be winners, too.

Controversy and Conflict

We are reflecting an image of Christ. The problem with many believers is our mistaken idea of who Y'shua is. We've heard so many hymns of the "child meek and mild" that we forget the person who stands up to the Pharisees and calls them whited sepulchers. We forget the superbly skilled debater. We forget the person who knows how to use a person's rules against him: "You tithe mint and cumin but neglect the weightier matters of the law." Spiritually speaking, we have to see Y'shua for who He is, embroiled in controversy and conflict.

***

The "natural man" wants to avoid controversy and conflict. The spiritual person knows that it's inevitable, even though she or he never enjoys it. We don't like to cause pain, and perhaps the impact of the gospel causes pain. That pain is momentary, but there's an even worse, eternal pain. We should not mute our proclamation in order to avoid impact. But we should sharpen it and focus it so it can cause impact at the right time, at the right place, in the right way.

***

If you want the general approval of society, don't be a missionary to the Jews. If you want the general approval of society, become a poet, write songs, become a performer, a teller of jokes, or a soother guilt feelings. Learn how to flatter people. The shallowness of this world causes people to want to surround themselves with flatterers. If you want to be liked, allow yourself to be manipulated by others who want to possess you and use you. But that's not you. We will be disliked by the world if we are doing our duty.

* * *

Concerning our opposition: When we're born again, God makes us like babies no matter what we were before. I'm convinced this is the reason it's so hard for the high and noble to come to the Lord. Because when you're born again, in a sense, you're a nobody, a beginner. Those who oppose the gospel don't want to become that helpless baby, to accept that role and the changes it requires.

The Cross

Concerning Calvary, I bow in awe at the thought, but I cringe sometimes at the flowery rhetoric we hear in sermons about the cross. I could never understand how anyone could describe a cross as beautiful. To me the symbol is as beautiful as a gas chamber or a hangman's noose. The cross was horrible, built to display the dying nakedness of a criminal, and intended to frighten and awe passersby with the grim reality of wrath, judgment and punishment. There is nothing beautiful about the cross or the blood that was shed on it, unless one has a perverted mind.

Yet God, who produced Creation from nothing, can produce beauty from ugliness. From the decaying carcass of a lion, God produced honey (Judges 14:8). From a marriage founded on duplicity and adultery, God raised up King Solomon (2 Samuel 12:24). From the horror of Calvary, God brings forth joy. With Y'shua's stripes He heals. Through the cross, that ugly instrument of judgment and death, He transforms believers. Through the shed blood of Christ, He covers our sin-stained lives with His righteousness—and adorns us with the beauty of His holiness.

* * *

There is no such thing as a comfortable cross, but the cross is the instrument of service—the way by which Y'shua served God the Father, the way by which He served humanity. It is the instrument by which the love of God is conveyed to us, and by taking up our cross daily to follow Him, whether we be scrubwomen or surgeons, we show our love for God. Everyone has to take up that cross.

By cross bearing, we testify of the grace of God. Those of us who are called to be evangelists must at all times exemplify the cross. Cross-bearing is not a joyless duty. It is at the core of ministry. The pain and anguish, joy and satisfaction exist together. Eventually, the pain and anguish fade and the joy and satisfaction survive within us, and the death of the flesh becomes the transition of the fullness of joy.

Debt

Don't buy things for your pleasure or for your convenience until you've paid your bills. You are not entitled to spend money for anything that you enjoy as long as you are in debt. When you are in debt you don't deserve to enjoy buying more things—you only deserve the opportunity to meet your obligations.

Dedication to God

The measure of a person's dedication to God is what they do for others, what they give for others—and how little they do for themselves and keep for themselves.

Defense Mechanisms

When confronted by unpleasant realities, people build structures, defense structures, which are in effect shields or blinders to keep us from seeing the unpleasant realities of life. But woe to those who start using the name of God for their defense mechanism because, in doing that, they are guilty of taking the name of the Lord in vain.

Dignity of Work

I believe in the dignity of labor; that working in itself is good. God forbid that any of us become "too good" to do what needs to be done. To have contempt for work is to have contempt for the worker. Most of us don't have a choice as to whether or not we're going to work. However, we do have a choice as to our attitude toward the work. Leaders, if you think you're too good or too important to pack boxes, you're sending a message to everyone you ask to pack those boxes. You're telling them that you have contempt for what they're doing. You never want to let yourself send that message.

Disappointment

Disappointment is a missed appointment. It means there is no convergence; things that were supposed to come together did not. Perhaps we missed the mark by setting our expectations too high; perhaps others missed the mark in what was understood to be an agreement. Perhaps the situation fell short of what was promised. Theologically or spiritually, disappointment is missing the appointed mark. We fall short of pleasing God. We also fall short of pleasing others and some fall short of pleasing us. We must have a regular time of scriptural reflection in order to realize when it is right to be disappointed in ourselves or others.

When we disappoint God, ourselves, or those who had a right to expect more from us, we need to repent. But what about the disappointments we feel from others?

When you relate your disappointment through the filter of the cross, a disappointment can be an opportunity. In the cross, we already reckon ourselves as dead to the things of this world. How can one disappoint a dead person? The operative verse in dealing with our own disappointments should be **Galatians 2:20**: "I have been crucified with Christ; it is no longer I who live, but Christ lives in me; and the *life* which I now live in the flesh I live by faith in the Son of God, who loved me and gave Himself for me."

This is the greater reality I've been talking about. You're dead people. If you are dead then everything good you experience is a bonus and every disappointment is a petty annoyance. When people disappoint you, if you are responsible to supervise them, you have to help them do better with sticking to their commitments. But if you are crucified with Christ, you don't let your disappointment turn to resentment.

***

Perhaps nothing is as devastating to one's morale as a disappointing coworker who was once part of your team. Sometimes their "work becomes 'shirk.'" Sometimes they quit the team altogether and make the rest of the players feel like losers. When a coworker leaves, one always feels lonely. And because there's more for each of us to do, the loneliness turns to disappointment.

Sometimes disappointment turns to grief when we see people head away from the place of grace and decline to practice the faith. We wonder how they could have affirmed our commitments, stood with us, taken the disapproval that we took, prayed fervently to the Lord—because now it seems to mean nothing to them. But it is good to remember that God is not through working with people even when they quit us and seem to quit Him.

Whatever you do for someone, whatever you give to them, do it and give it as unto the Lord. Do it for Jesus, not merely for the person. If you base what you do and give on your relationship with the Lord, you are motivated by the only One who will not let you down. Even if your relationship with a person is devastated, what you did and what you gave has value. It stands as a sacrifice to the Lord.

***

Cross-centered disappointments are always appointments for growth. Me-centered disappointments can be harvests of emptiness.

***

Some people are perpetually getting angry because that is the way they choose to deal with every disappointment and every hurt. Their anger somehow allows them to feel in control. You can choose to feel offended by what someone said, you can choose to be angry, or you can choose not to be angry. Maybe not all the time, but choosing what we think and feel is a discipline that improves with practice. If you want to try it, make a three-by-five card with the text of Philippians 4:8 printed on it.

> Finally, brethren, whatever things are true, whatever things *are* noble, whatever things *are* just, whatever things *are* pure, whatever things *are* lovely, whatever things *are* of good report, if *there is* any virtue and if *there is* anything praiseworthy—meditate on these things.

Put it in your pocket, your wallet, or your purse. Meditate on it, pray about it. When you find yourself beginning to dwell on thoughts or feelings that should not characterize a child of God, pull out that card. Ask God to shape those thoughts and those feelings to something more worthy.

Enduring

Don't let what you don't have be a focal point of your life. Whatever you have on this earth, you're really not going to be here all that long. If you haven't already, you will reach the point where it isn't just the years but the decades that are going by pretty quickly. That should not depress you because when your years here are finished, you are going to be with the Lord, and the good things you have now are just a foreshadowing of what is to come for all eternity.

And likewise, whatever you are missing, you won't be missing for all that long. And if you can endure doing without as unto the Lord, instead of complaining about it, someday you're going to hear Him say, "Well done, good and faithful servant." And that will be sweeter by far than whatever it was that you did without during your brief stay on this earth.

***

It is in the testing and trials of life that we develop our best skills. We discover our strengths. We learn how to handle situations and see the value of our principles. Whereas we wish trouble on no one, it usually serves to make good people better and make better people the best. Ignoble or wicked people become more desperate in their evil attitudes and imaginings during trials, whereas those who have been made righteous by Christ wear suffering as a crown to the glory of God.

***

Sometimes we can be dazzled by the world so that God's will becomes dimmed, but when all is darkness around us the light of God brightens our paths.

Evangelism

Old sayings like "You can catch more flies with honey than with vinegar" are all right if you want to catch flies, but we're not out to catch flies. If you want to be safe, you want to have sanctuary, go to church. The only way a local church is ever going to be very effective in evangelism is if number one, the pastor is an example of going out personally to do evangelism, and number two, the people are willing to take risks. People won't do evangelism until they understand and accept that they won't get promoted at work because they talk "religion" too much. Their neighbors might dislike them, and the only ones who will ever really understand and appreciate them are other Christians who are actively sharing their faith and those whose hearts God has touched to receive the gospel message.

***

In talking to people about how to witness, the first thing it's important for them to know is they don't have to be liked to be a good witness.

The second thing to tell them is God won't let you fail even if you seem to fail.

The discovery of a truth which shows us our own inadequacy is never a joyous event. That's why we resist the preaching of the gospel, since the message of salvation we bring must include the news that all are lost without a savior. We don't want to discover any truth that says we've been doing things wrong up until now. But when we allow ourselves to see that we are wrong, we have the joy of being made right.

***

Some believe it's necessary to establish a relationship in which the other person notices certain qualities or characteristics in them *before* they mention Christ. This would be difficult for the true, committed Christian, because Christ isn't in the back of our minds, the back of our hearts. If we are just being ourselves, we can't help but speak of Him, and what He's doing for us. So much of what we have and what we're able to do is because of the empowerment of Christ, so it is the normal, natural thing for Him to be part of many discussions. That doesn't mean you should be sanctimonious or constantly make religion a topic of discussion. It means be yourself.

If we accept a relationship or a friendship on the basis that we will not "bother the other person with religion" until they ask, then we're flying a false flag. We are *not* like everyone else and if we are honest, people will know where we stand. Yet, one can speak of the gospel, mention Christ, show respect and uphold Him in such a way that other people can see it but can also know that they are respected, loved and appreciated. I don't think one could know a devout Muslim a half day without realizing that the person had a commitment to pray at certain times. I don't think that one could have a meal with a Buddhist and fail to realize that because of his religion, he won't eat certain foods. The strong convictions of most people aren't far below the surface, and we don't help ourselves or others by seeking to hide our own convictions until people have accepted us.

Excuses

If you make a mistake, and you know it is a mistake and you tell me about it, it is forgiven. Do the same with your subordinates. Do not allow excuses. Allowing excuses encourages a person to lie. We can always find reasons (excuses) to stop us from doing a duty we don't want to do, and it's not unusual for people to practice a certain degree of self-deception to come to this reason.

***

Some give excuses instead of explanations and some give explanations that are really excuses. I usually don't accept excuses and usually don't require explanations. One of my axioms is, "Don't bother making excuses. Everyone makes mistakes. If you don't make mistakes often, you don't need excuses, and if you do make mistakes often, no excuse will do."

***

It is a social ritual to allow imperfect people to maintain a perfect face. The "explanation-excuse syndrome" and its acceptance as a social ritual is damaging because it paints the motivation of a perpetrator with the color of purity that no one has.

Faithfulness

Being faithful is taking a direction towards a destiny; it is trotting a path directed toward God's will and God's ways.

***

Cynicism is the enemy of faith and faithfulness.

***

Some think that faithfulness is simply enduring to the end, doing what you ought to do and being what you ought to be no matter how you feel about it. There is a certain amount of truth to that, but that view doesn't take into account the fact that faithfulness can change, not only how you feel about yourself, but it can actually change your character so that you can be the very best you. That's what faithfulness does for you.

***

Our goal is not merely to *behave* in a certain way, but to *be* more like Jesus. Therefore, the standards to which we commit ourselves not only include what we do, but how we think and feel—because the Bible tells us, "As a man thinks, so he *is*." Faithfulness must extend to our thoughts and feelings because both move us either toward or away from being godly people.

***

Sometimes we feel spiritually dry even when we have been relating to the Lord properly: confessing sin, reading His word and seeking Him in prayer. Somehow we just can't sense His reality. But we can, by faith, be led of the Spirit. Sometimes to function in the absence of feelings strengthens our association with the Lord.

It's not unlike human relationships, where we don't always feel what we want to feel toward those whom we love. We don't ignore our loved ones in the absence of those feelings, but rather we need to continue relating to them on the basis of our commitment not on our current feelings. That is a lot of being faithful. God wants us to be faithful to Him. And the wonderful thing is, He never ceases being faithful to us.

Fitting in

We need to be creatively maladjusted men and women who do not fit in because we refuse to bow down to the idols of this world: materialism, self-seeking, and pride.

William Wilberforce was an example of the right kind of maladjustment. He was a rather unspectacular Member of Parliament in 18th-century Britain. He felt that God's overriding purpose in bringing him into Parliament was to abolish the slave trade.

As he lobbied for such legislation, the government accused him of plotting the financial suicide of the British Empire. After 20 years of labor which destroyed Wilberforce's health, reputation, and financial security, a bill passed abolishing the slave trade in Britain and 20 million pounds were paid out of the treasury to the trade victims. (It was estimated at the time that the slave trade had destroyed 20 million lives.) This act has been called "one of the two or three totally righteous acts of government in human history."

***

I'd rather be liked than disliked. I'd rather be loved than hated. I'd rather tell a person that he or she is right than that they are wrong. I'd rather fit in than stand apart. I recognize that in myself, and I fight it within myself. You must fight it within you. You are *not* ordinary. You're not just like everybody else. You are the called of God. You are chosen. He wants to use you. That means that you are going to be an oddball because true Christianity is and always has been a counter-culture.

Fools

Sometimes fools are very bright people. However, they are brittle, rigid, and they know only what they know (or think they know) and are not willing to know any more. The problem with fools is that they are sure that they know enough and think that they are all that they should be.

Forgiveness

Oftentimes people ask for forgiveness when they want to be excused. When asking for forgiveness, a person who has wronged someone needs to think through how they can offer to make it right. While it is true that God forgives us because of His grace, Scripture is also very clear about people making restitution when they wrong one another.

Also, there are those who use the concept of forgiveness as a sanctimonious way to complain. "Please forgive me because I've harbored anger against you" might be a sincere statement, but too often it is the prelude to a person venting their anger. You find that people are asking you for forgiveness when what they really want is an apology from you. Maybe you need to apologize, but it's a manipulative way to go about getting an apology.

***

We are able to forgive people who deny us or let us down because we know that we have denied others and have let them down. I don't know about you, but what makes it easy for me to forgive is that I've been forgiven so much by other people. Even more, by our actions we've denied the Lord and have let Him down. Because He's forgiven us we can forgive others.

Friends

I decided I would not let my friends happen to me. I would choose them to become my friends and do the work of being a friend to gain them as friends, colleagues and companions.

Giving

Your own donations show what you believe. You can't expect anyone else to support our ministry financially if you aren't doing the same.

Goals

One way of setting goals is to take a personal inventory of all God has given you—then set goals according to how you want to invest what He has entrusted to you.

***

How do you set goals? First, you have to do the things that you are requiring others to do and you must be able to do them right.

Goals are important because you have to let people know what you expect. If goals are too high, and people reach as hard as they can but can't reach the goals, you devastate them. However, sometimes when a reasonable goal is set, people stop working as soon as they reach the minimum that is acceptable.

Don't be afraid of admitting failure; it is important to call a failure a failure. Without a failure line, we lose our lower reference point from which to gauge success and victory lines.

***

When we set goals, we test ourselves as leaders and also the hearts and loyalty of our subordinates.

God's Leading

Usually when I've had God's direct leading, it was not to anything that gave me more status, or more enjoyment, or more of anything except grief. I naturally gravitate toward those things which give me more status and more pleasure. I needed God's direct leading to those things that were His will that gave me grief.

God's Sovereignty

God simply does not give us reasons for everything He does. We must remember who is accountable to whom. Theology is not a study of divine behavior, so much as it is a study of our ideas about God's nature based on our observations of His dealings with humanity. God has explained enough for us to trust Him and His goodness. Yet no amount of divine explanation would serve to convince those who are determined to remain in their unbelief.

If God is not good, there is no such thing as good. If God, the ultimate Authority, is not allowed to do what He wants, where He wants, whenever He wants, then what rights do *we*, His creatures, have?

God never said to anyone, "Pardon me for intruding on your life." But so far as I'm concerned, He can interrupt me—tell me something, change my direction—anytime He wants to. After all, no matter what I am involved in doing, I am really just on call in His service. He doesn't need to answer to me. I must answer to Him.

Hardship

I like this room [speaking of the large attic room where council meetings were held]. It's true that the rafters are unfinished and a little rough, but what I like about this room are the skylights and the way they let the light in. Our lives are like that. There's a roughness, but the roughness puts us in a place where light can enter.

Hardship is something to which we have to commit ourselves. Not that we're going to seek unneeded hardships, but we have to commit ourselves to enduring hardship because the best opportunities are often found in the rough places.

***

Dear friends, beloved of God, God has a toll of grief, a toll of pain for each of you to bear. Some of that pain is disappointment in yourselves and your abilities. Some of that pain is disappointment in your families. And some of that pain is disappointment in the people to whom you minister. Who hasn't seen a bright light, a shining testimony, flicker, grow dim and go out? Do you sorrow? Do you grieve when it happens? I grieve.

Impulses

A disciplined person doesn't act on impulse, though he or she might have as many or more impulses than someone we call impulsive. There are big impulses and small impulses. There is the impulse to tell someone to "shut up," or the impulse to take the last cookie on the plate. Or, there is the impulse, when a task is described to say, "I'll do that. I'll take care of it." Or the impulse to give everything we have to a particular mission or cause.

A mature person reviews each and every impulse and decides to act on some, partially act on others and resist the rest altogether. But in the mature person, there's a fourth possibility, and that is to defer an impulse and deal with it when it's appropriate. Part of discipline is choosing to be with people who know who you are and will help you control your impulses. Even so, every individual is ultimately responsible for how they allow themselves to feel and react when faced with their own impulses.

Intuition

Intuition is not mystical. It is the subconscious recognizing data and determining meaning before the conscious mind can work on it.

Investing in People

Be more attentive to the little ones, the new missionaries and especially your own children. Missionaries come and go, but your spouse and children will be with you the rest of your life and they're worth putting a lot of time into. Most of what you're going to get won't be from your staff members or buddies, but from your spouse and children.

Everyone here with families needs to understand the same thing. Most of what a person is going to get from life won't be from staff, but from their own families. When I talk about "getting" I'm not just talking about *nachas* (a pride and joy). I learn from my children and my wife. I would not be a writer today if I didn't have a wife who loves words and who is intolerant of non-grammatical language. I have been strengthened by a lot of other people. But the one who has strengthened me the most is my wife, and I learn things from my daughters all the time. As a parent gives himself to his or her children, as he or she gives information and experiences, the children will become givers. And eventually the parents will receive from their children.

Jews for Jesus Ministry Mindset

These excerpts show what Moishe believed a mission should be, and how missionaries should think and act.

We have never considered ourselves an organization in the usual sense of the term. We are far more than an organization. We are far more than an institution. We are a society, or a community, committed to the Lord and one another.

***

We'll not be able to stay on the frontlines if we continue to tell the gospel the way we told it ten years ago. The message has not changed but the conveyance of the message and the medium of the message must be ever new and renewed, speaking to each month, each year, each event with a message for "now."

***

We don't encourage people to be foolhardy, but faith must replace fear in a ministry mind-set.

***

We need to be people who are willing to die for the Lord, people who want to live for the Lord, who want to serve the Lord and who want to defy society.

***

I like the rebels of this world, the counter-culture groups. I feel that God established Israel to be a counter-culture in the world, and that the church has often failed to be a counter-culture.

***

Loyalty to Jews for Jesus should never cause you to begrudge or belittle the successes of other ministries.

***

Anyone who is honestly and honorably engaged in Jewish evangelism is our friend. Whether or not they have discovered that we are their friends is irrelevant. If you have reason to believe they have badmouthed us, continue to uphold them. We are not competing with them; we are competing against what we could be. We will work with anyone who will work with us.

***

Sandstone cannot sharpen anything because it will turn to sand. Flint, on the other hand, can cut because it is a hard stone. We live in an age where believers have soft faces and hard hearts. But we want to have soft hearts and hard faces. When we come up against obstacles, we want to break through them. The soft-faced believers seem open and interested, but their hearts are afar off and you cannot touch them. Loving is done, not with the face, but with the heart.

***

When determining what is acceptable, do not be manipulated by incompetence. There is a certain tendency which we will not accept: "Presuming on Grace." In other words, "Anything goes if you are sincere." According to that mind-set, the big sin is hurting someone's feelings. If you maintain quality standards, and insist on those standards, those who presume on grace call you a legalist. Yet they enjoy the benefits of the standards you have set. It is our duty to set high standards and to hold ourselves and those who work with us to those standards.

***

Is it true that if we get people to like us they will get saved? No. People who are seeking God are the ones who get saved. They get saved and discipled and then they go off feeling that they owe us nothing. But if we are doing our work for the Lord and His glory, that's all right. When we serve people because we love God, they *don't* owe us anything.

***

You are God's gift to the world when you minister for Him. You do not have the right to take yourself back. You'll ruin God's reputation!

***

We cannot allow ourselves to be enticed or seduced by the comforts of this world so that we commit ourselves to our own comfort. This is not to say that we should not allow ourselves any comforts, but they should always be ancillary to our main purpose. We are a cause-oriented group and unless we step forward with Jesus as our continuing cause we will go into the ordinary mode of dealing with those who come to us instead of going out to reach others.

***

Ministry is like marriage. You're always married. Wherever you go, there are certain things that a person can and can't do because he or she is married. It would be inappropriate for you as ministers to relate as though you were like everyone else when in fact you're not.

Leadership

Some people demand too much of a leader's attention, approval and affection; others behave like just having you exist over them is a nuisance which they tolerate. But no matter how they respond or react to your leadership, that does not change your duty to them. No matter how they behave, you owe them something. When we are leading people, we give them more when we challenge them to be more for God, to do more for God.

***

A leader helps the staff be flexible and prepares them for change. However, a responsible leader will not change an established policy without a great deal of thought and staff preparation.

***

There is always the dialectic tension between those who lead and those who follow the leader. To behave as though tension does not exist between leaders and those who are led is folly.

***

When leaders are successful in training those under them to be disciples, the subordinates won't need the leaders as much, and they'll rise above their leaders. They'll discover things on their own. The leader won't need to exhort, reprove or rebuke the subordinates nearly as much. Instead they will have a blessed fellowship together.

***

Be patient with beginners. Teach them by their mistakes, but never accept the mistakes as that which ought to be. Expect your people to grow.

***

In being models for others, we've got to criticize ourselves openly; we've got to be ready to say what's wrong about ourselves so others won't follow us in our wrongness.

Learning

If you can't learn from those you're teaching then you're not much of a teacher. As long as you regard yourself as being a canon, a beholder of the truth, a complete person, you're obsolete.

***

There is more out there than anybody could ever know. Whatever age you are, there is still a lot to learn. Watch out for those who behave like they know it all and have experienced everything. Beware of those who are seeking mastery over all knowledge and all experience.

***

When some of you reach for something, you snatch at things not knowing that you're welcome to the table to pick up whatever you want. When it comes to thinking, you're a snatcher when you could be walking away with a whole basketful of things from the table.

Love

If you love somebody, whether it's your spouse, or your children or your friends, don't take their cross away from them. Stand by, and comfort them, but let them carry it.

***

We either love in response to what is right, because we've made a decision to love, or we love in response to our own needs, in which case, it's not love at all, but a form of lust.

***

A small heart is a crowded heart; a big heart has room to do something for God, for family, for friends.

* * *

There are some people who derive power from causing you distress. You cannot love these people the way they want to be loved, because the way they want to be loved is for you to present yourself as an object of their aggression. That is not love, because it encourages a behavior that is not of benefit to them. To love is to position oneself so as to be of benefit to one's beloved.

Management

The most important tool in management is time knowledge. A manager does not need to know how to perform every function, but he does need to know how much time it takes and what it costs.

* * *

The last part of a job is to properly report it. A manager who does not require a report on the work but says, "I trust you" is a lazy manager.

Marriage

For the newly married, it is a shock to discover how imperfect the union of two sinners can be. That doesn't mean that marriage is not a good thing. I believe in marriage, and it was created for good. I'm glad I'm married and I'm glad many of you are married. Those of you who got married wanted a good thing, and those of you who are single and want marriage want a good thing—but that doesn't mean that in all cases, marriage is the best thing for you. A bad marriage is worse than a relatively good single life.

Husbands, some of your wives complain that you don't talk to them enough. Where is the rule book that says how much is "enough"? Are fifteen sentences a day enough? Are twenty paragraphs? But your wives are not talking about "talk." They're saying, "Pay some attention to me." And they have the right to say that.

***

More than talking to your spouse, it's important to make an agreement with yourself to be available and attend to him or her. Maybe it's just a matter of sitting in the kitchen while your spouse is cooking or repairing something. You might not even be talking. But it means not going someplace else and busying yourself with something else at that time. That way if you or your spouse have something to say, you're within talking range of each other.

***

Many seem to feel that singleness is just an imperfect state until marriage. Is singleness an imperfect state? The answer is yes, but so is marriage. You need to see: All of existence is an imperfect state until Jesus returns. Whether you are married or single you will not be complete until that day.

There is no spiritual or biblical justification for regarding single people as being incomplete any more than married people. This was the case for Adam, but Adam was unique. He and his wife were the only people who ever experienced marriage *within the context of an unhindered relationship with God*. In the beginning, their fellowship with God was not marred by sin. They alone were actually capable of living as completed and completely fulfilled human beings.

That is no longer possible. Two people cannot complete one another because whether we are single or married, we are still incomplete in terms of our fellowship with God. And that incompleteness also affects our human relationships, because a person who needs more of the Lord cannot give exactly as they should to their spouse. The quality of marriage depends on both partners' relationship with God. Usually one or the other spouse is going to be doing better with their walk at a given time. When one partner is struggling with the Lord, no matter how well the other partner is doing, the quality of the marriage is lessened.

Marriage is not the happy ending to a single life. It is the beginning of a new life with uncharted ground. The happy ending does not come until our transformation is finished and our relationship with God is perfected.

* * *

Some people stop relating to their single friends when they get married. That is like telling them, "Now that I've found my real life and my true destiny, I don't need you anymore." To such a person I would say two things. First, your friends didn't stop needing you just because you got married. And second, you do not stop needing friendships outside your marriage. It is unrealistic to expect your spouse to be all your friends rolled into one. That is putting an undue burden on the marriage. Any spouse who wants wife or husband to need only him or her (and maybe their children) does not understand enough about love to be a very good partner.

Unfortunately, some newly married people have a tendency to drop friendships without realizing it. Just remember that marriage should widen the circle of people in your life, not narrow it. Make a conscious effort to include people. It is natural for newlyweds to be preoccupied with one another. But if you leave your other friendships in limbo when you get married, you can't expect to come back later and resume them on the same level.

* * *

Married people, if you want to extol the virtues of marriage, do it by the exemplary way you treat your spouse. And don't think that single people don't see or care how you treat one another. They may or may not want what you have.

To assume that everyone wants or needs what you have is snobbery. Marriage-snobbery is wrong. It is based on pride and prejudice. If you are married, you should not presume to treat single people as though they are incapable of understanding situations or reaching a level of maturity unless or until they experience what you have experienced. It is true that there are people who don't grow and mature until they are stretched by marriage and parenthood. But that is not all people. God is not limited in the ways that He chooses to develop us.

Single-snobbery is also wrong. If you have the strength to remain single and content, be careful that you do not judge those who are married or who would like to be married by your own experience. A settled single can be a great help and support to single people who are uncertain as to whether they will ever marry. But great sensitivity must be exercised. No one ought to tell someone who truly desires marriage, "You're better off single."

Offenses

We must distinguish between actual offenses and the posture of being offended. Some people choose to be offended as a way of manipulating others. The cross will always be an offense. Ask a person who expresses that they are offended to help you understand why they feel they should be offended. If the explanation is reasonable, and you see that you have done wrong, apologize. On the other hand, in dealing with pretended offenses where the person shouldn't have been offended, don't apologize.

***

What do you do if you know you have offended someone? Don't make excuses. Even if the dog ate your school paper, you still don't have it. Even if the fire truck was in your way so that you could not get by, if you're late, you're late. Telling a person the reason why only exacerbates the problem because in effect you are saying they must accept what you've done because of the circumstances. "I'm sorry" means "I did wrong" or "I was inadequate." If you started out ten minutes earlier, maybe the fire truck being in your way wouldn't really matter. If you'd fed the dog, maybe he wouldn't have eaten your paper.

When you know you have offended someone you should do three things:

1. Apologize. Admit that you've done wrong.
2. Ask for forgiveness from the people that you've wronged.
3. Ask what you might do to rectify the situation.

Separate the three. Saying "I'm sorry" doesn't change things. Asking for forgiveness recognizes that you have wronged somebody or cost them something. But the Bible says that we must bring forth fruits for repentance. And one must always say, "What can I do to make this right?" Here is a good way to put it: "I can't for the world give you back the twenty minutes of your time that I wasted. What can I do to make it right? Maybe you would let me pay for our meal." Make a suggestion.

***

If those whom you supervise behave like they are offended you've got to deal with them patiently. After all, they're staff and you've got some commitment to them. You must sit them down and follow a line of questioning. Usually, by asking a person a series of questions, people will either come to the truth or come to the end of themselves.

Opportunities

As much as you would like to believe it, few real opportunities come knocking on your door. If somebody approaches you with a business idea that involves you, there's a good chance that it's their business and to their profit, and they see you as the consumer or user. The real opportunities are out there but they are doors on which you have to knock.

***

When you pray for someone to have opportunities, pray that they'll have energy, initiative, and creativity. Pray that they might be able to see an opportunity and to know a true opportunity from a false opportunity. Pray that they might be diligent in following through when doors of opportunity are presented.

Opposition

We must be aware of efforts to undermine our reputation. But we must not be defensive, nor should we attack the character of those who attack us. Rather we need to develop more personal relationships with those who will support us if they see that we are credible people, sensitive people who are thoughtfully trying to do the right thing.

Parenting

It is wrong for parents to withdraw their guidance and teaching before their children are grown. And not to withdraw it [at least to some degree] after they're grown also is wrong. There should come a time when parents gradually withdraw their fostering, teaching and protecting. If the parents do not, they will damage the child. The parents must teach their children what they need to know to guide their own lives at a time when they can assimilate it.

***

The joy of being a parent is letting go when your children no longer need you as a parent but want to relate to you as a friend. There's no more obligation on their part to listen to what you have to say. Yet they seek you out because they feel you still have something to say to them as adults. It is a joy when they want to associate with you because of pleasant association in the past, not out of obligation.

***

I made a commitment that in an emergency, my children could count on me. No matter when or where, I was interruptible. They didn't need that very often, but I tried to be approachable.

***

How blessed is a child who gains self-discipline at an early age and knows how to control him- or herself. Sometimes when our children get into mischief and we behave like they are cute, we encourage them to follow their bad impulses. We need to hold them responsible when they do what is wrong and when they fail to do what is right. We need to teach them that self-control is possible and necessary.

Pentecost

The message of Pentecost is that God's presence provides God's power. When the Holy Spirit came, the disciples did not remain in the upper room, nor did they try to enshrine their experience within sanctuary walls. They took to the streets where the people were. Those who had never before "witnessed" found themselves proclaiming the wonderful works of God in languages they had never learned, with a boldness they had never possessed. The results were electric! Those who heard were polarized by the charge of the Holy Spirit, and spiritual sparks flew to ignite revival in receptive hearts.

At Pentecost, Jews living as aliens in many countries had come to Jerusalem to celebrate that pilgrim festival. When the

Pentecost event happened and they became charged with the electricity of the Holy Spirit, they did not linger at Jerusalem where the current flowed most strongly. They did not send letters home to their relatives and friends inviting them to come to the happening. They brought the happening back with them. And the power imparted by God at Pentecost manifested itself through their witness to those around them. Those who had received that power began to turn the world upside down.

Today many churches tend to regard their congregations and religious gatherings the way the ancient Hebrews regarded the Temple at Jerusalem—as God's official headquarters. This inaccurate interpretation leads to ineffectual evangelism. No church building or church gathering is God's headquarters. The Holy Spirit has made each believing heart His headquarters—His command post, from which He may conduct His campaign for us to win others. As yielded believers, we are mobile units awaiting His instructions. At His command we are to go forward, energized and enabled by His power. That's real go power, the dynamo that can make us effective evangelists.

Persecution

"Every knock is a boost" if you know how to receive it. What we must do is to use "spiritual judo" to learn to take the blow in the right place so that we can use the energy from it to accomplish our purposes.

***

I've drawn the aphorism "Every knock is a boost" from the life of Joseph who was used to redeem his brothers after they'd sold him into slavery to the Egyptians. Joseph's trouble became an occasion for God to work. In the end, when he finally confronts his brothers and reveals his true identity and they have great fear, he tells them most graciously, "You intended this for evil but God intended it for good." Trouble is like that. Oppression, aggression, illness, whatever we encounter can work to the glory of God, to our benefit and to the benefit of others.

Personal Ethics

There are ethics of society and organization ethics, but it is also important to have your own personal ethics. Each of us has to act alone in private situations that test our ethics. When those test times and trying situations come, how you handle temptation will depend in large part on your own personal ethical code.

You need to know that you gain strength from exercising or operating your own principles under the supervision of the Holy Spirit. Those are key words when seen together: operate and principle. The moral muscle you build by operating your principles is used by God to empower you and enable you to deal with situations before they arise—so you don't have to start searching to find those inner resources at the crucial moment of testing. They are immediately before you as policies and principles under which you normally operate.

Without personal ethics, you will not be able to uphold the ethics of the church or the ministry in that moment of testing, when there is no one present to witness your choice. It is not enough to be accountable to other people. In that lonely moment of testing, you have got to be accountable to yourself as one who controls self and is accountable to God. Even God does not make you do things His way in that moment. You have to answer to yourself and support the decisions you have made about the person you want to be. That is why it is so important that each one of us think and decide very carefully about our own, individual, very personal ethics.

***

Without ethics, people generally move toward their goal in whatever way presents itself or seems likely to get results. People are apt, at some point, to take questionable shortcuts to reach their goals. They may rationalize that "the ends justify the means" or that they are choosing the "lesser of two evils." Ethics protects against those kinds of traps because it takes into account the means as well as the ends.

When we subscribe to a system of ethics, we are disciplining ourselves, restricting ourselves to being and doing according to certain standards. When we choose a Christlike aim, we automatically exclude ourselves from an "ends justify the means" type of ethic. We cannot separate the means from the ends! Both the means and the ends are opportunities to conform to or distort the character of God . . . to obey or disobey God . . . to follow Y'shua's example or depart from it.

***

Note that the Bible does not define "right" as the means to happiness or to a lack of harm, though Scriptures certainly do point out the blessings that often correspond to right behavior. But that which is right or good is to be desired for itself.

***

Personal ethics entail your commitment to standards that enable you to achieve your honorable aims and purposes. They are principles which translate into personal policies and are applied as personal procedures.

Some of you have personal ethics, decisions and commitments you've made at various points in your life—but you've never looked at them as a body of principles, or realized that what you were doing was building an ethical system.

Others of you have not realized that it is up to you to make these decisions for yourself. You know you are supposed to be godly, but you haven't taken specific steps, made specific commitments to keep you from ungodly behavior. Some might think you don't need to take such steps when you've got the Holy Spirit. But consider this. When the Lord gave us the Holy Scriptures, in His infinite wisdom, He filled it with examples of godly people who stumbled and made mistakes. Yes, when we receive Jesus we have the Holy Spirit, but none of us walks according to the Spirit every moment of our lives—and we won't until God has finished the work He began in each of us. Until then, you had better have a system of personal ethics to fall back on.

We can provide ministry ethics. But without the personal ethics of each one of you to uphold them, they will be merely institutional. Your ethics are your own personal tool. If you forge them carefully and prayerfully, they can be an exceedingly valuable tool.

Personality and Skills

Personality refers to the quality or qualities of an individual. Skill refers to proficiency or degree of deftness in performing a certain task. There is some overlap in personality and skills because godly qualities of being often translate into actions.

Most people understand that one doesn't acquire skills without discipline, practice . . . effort. But what most people do not understand is that the same can be true (to a degree) of personality. We can choose to develop certain qualities in addition to or instead of qualities which come naturally to us.

Planning, Long Term

Planning is like laying tracks. Once you've got the railroad track laid to a certain destination, unless you get derailed, you've got to that place. But our future is in opportunities; we've got to keep our flexibility.

I don't know what it will be like ten years from now, but I do know that if we plan too much, we will miss opportunities. First, we must plan to keep our eyes open to the opportunities. Annual witnessing campaigns, holiday services, etc. have become routine so unless we plan NOT to have them, they are part of our regular obligation.

We plan to have obligations. When we meet all of our obligations, we still have 40 percent of our work time free to take advantage of opportunities.

Praise

Be very careful where you collect friends, and never go back to the watering hole where praise was abundant for you, because you'll never get away from it. The thirst for praise becomes too important.

Prayer

When you pray, "continue earnestly in prayer, being vigilant in it with thanksgiving" as it says in Colossians 4:2. Thanksgiving does two things. First, it makes you aware of what God has done in the past. We constantly have to be reminded. But prayer with thanksgiving is not merely thanksgiving for the past; it is thanking God for hearing our prayers and whatever petition we might be bringing before Him now. We don't commemorate past events as we look to the future. Therefore, prayer with thanksgiving is prayer with hope.

***

I don't know if it's a Jewish thing, but I have found myself talking to God the way that Tevye from "Fiddler on the Roof" did. I have found myself complaining to God, saying things like, "So you think I need this?" Now, when I stop to think about it, I realize that whatever came from God was something He knew I needed, but the idea of talking back was partly an acknowledgement that He was there. The

Bible says, "Pray without ceasing." I always imagined wherever you go, you go with God and He's there, a kind of silent partner. When you need Him, you can look to Him and He gives a nod or sends "His signal."

Preaching

In the course of a worship service, give people as much Scripture as they'll stand for. God's Word is better than any sermon you can give if you can only get people to listen to it.

***

Don't ever get so caught up in your message that you stop seeing who you're preparing that message for and what those people need.

***

You're not preaching yourselves, you're preaching Christ, and don't forget it!

Principles

I have always been slow. When something would happen, I did not react right away; it took me a while to think about it. When I was a kid, if someone hit me, I would stand for a moment wondering if it was a fight or if he was trying to play a game. What were we supposed to be fighting about, or what were we supposed to be playing? So from an early age, I knew I needed to think things through ahead of time, so that when something happened, I would know what to do. And I didn't know that what I was doing was deciding on and living by principles.

Principles are decisions made in advance of how we will act. You have to establish your principles before people or situations confront you with how you will act. At the same time, these decisions will only stand if you have the desire and the determination to make them a part of who you are.

* * *

A rule doesn't mean that you may do it when it's convenient. A rule is to especially apply at those times when it is inconvenient.

* * *

Kindness doesn't preclude standards.

* * *

Once the principle is established, and we know we can stick to that principle, and it's firm, then we can start making exceptions. But when we make an exception, we have to know why we made that exception, rather than allowing an exception because we were careless. The exception has to be the result of a carefully weighed decision.

Renoir was trained as a classical artist before he started doing impressionistic paintings. He was capable of doing representational paintings. He could and did do representational portraits for money. He painted ordinary landscapes, and then, once he had the groundwork laid, he went off and started doing impressionistic work. But he didn't do impressionistic work to avoid the discipline of representational painting. We have too many people who will avoid the classic disciplines to cut their own groove, and they could never stay in a regular groove.

* * *

This is not a personality-centered organization, and it never will be. It's a principle and policy centered organization. As long as you stick to the principles, as long as you know them, and as long as you follow them, then I'm virtually irrelevant to your life and ministry. You're not going to hear a lot from me except for some occasional cheering. But where you don't know the principles and you need to know them, or you do know them and have decided to do something else, that's when I need to step in.

***

There are organizational principles, and within the organization people also need to have personal principles. We all make mistakes, and if we learn from those mistakes a principle often emerges. But there are times when learning from a mistake is just going to be too costly—and I don't mean cost in terms of mere money, though mistakes often do cost money. They also cost time, energy, and emotional resources. If you arrive at all your principles through making mistakes, you are going to be bankrupt. You've got to find a cheaper tuition.

Questions

The value of any question is twofold: to elicit information and to get the person thinking with you. A dishonorable use of the question is to ask a question when you only want to show what you know (or think you know).

Reality

In order to maintain comfort and a feeling of control, we humans tend to create for ourselves small spheres of unreality. The topography of the planet that revolves around us has oceans of small concerns, mountains of small but diversionary recreations, and the continents of our soul become connected by tenuous and transitory relationships. But that planet of self rotates and spins on an axis of excuses and untruths. We fail to realize that we're planets headed on a collision course with one another, and that tragedies large and small are raining like meteors into our atmosphere.

God enables us to endure the unpleasant, unfriendly realities of now. When we know Him, we understand that though reality can be harsh, its tragedies are but momentary, its pains are passing away for the greater reality of eternal life.

***

We need to commit ourselves to the fact that reality with Christ is not only endurable, but it's durable. We need to learn to crave truth, to relish what is real and to reject all obstacles that keep us from reaching that reality.

Rebellion

The rebellious person's heart becomes set against those to whom he is submitted and he or she begins to act accordingly. Is rebellion justified? When it is, we call it a revolution. Revolutions are sometimes justified. But remember that a revolution always destroys the structure. Before a person revolts, he or she must ask, "Am I sure that what I can bring into existence is better than what I am tearing down?" The interesting thing about rebellion is, many see themselves as revolutionaries simply because they were able to destroy the structure. But more often than not, it is not a revolution in the positive sense of building something better; rebellion is more often the destruction of a relationship and the destruction of trust.

***

When you break rules that were established to uphold you, you destroy your structure. You cannot be upheld by a structure that you didn't help support.

Recruiting

Most of you who are leaders are here in one way or another because I reached out to you. And when I did, I saw something in you that wasn't yet apparent to everyone else. If you're building staff, look for the people you can help gain achievement. Watch for "comers," not for people who have arrived.

***

When you consider people for staff and volunteers, they should be people who are capable of getting excited about God. You can't fake it. Either that sense of reality is there for a person, or it's not.

When we talk about dedication, consecration, anointing, we're talking about a "sometimes" thing. No one is hitting that top level of dedication all the time, but you've got to see the potential. When you're looking to recruit a serious volunteer or staff person, first see whether or not they get excited about God. See if they get a little misty-eyed when you talk about God and what He does. Do they see it? Can they be motivated by it?

***

Look for people who do what's necessary without making a big deal out of it. When you send somebody to the store to buy Kleenex, if you have to explain which store to go to, how to get there, what size Kleenex to buy, how much to spend, where to get the money, whether or not to bring back the receipt, that person requires too much attention to get much done. Some people want to do five ounces of work for five pounds of attention. Look for people who do things with dispatch.

Relating to Others

Don't allow yourselves to become possessive of people. Don't call people to yourself. They are fellow travelers. Their road should lead to God, not to you.

***

Make people your own. That doesn't mean be possessive. When you say "my dad" you don't possess him anymore than he possesses you. It's a way of relating. That kind of ownership means you recognize obligation. Your dad or your child is yours to take care of, and if you do that in the proper way, people will recognize that you are theirs, too, to take care of, and to care for. That is different from possessiveness, which is merely coveting people.

***

Did you ever see a cow that lost its calf, or a dog that lost its puppies? The nipples become swollen and painful. I saw that happen to a dog once, and she didn't do anything but whimper for days. I thought she was mourning because one of her puppies died. I talked to the veterinarian who said it wasn't. He said dogs don't remember if they gave birth to one puppy or five. The dog just had too much milk. The veterinarian gave her a shot, which cured her very quickly.

The spiritual life is like the biological life. You've got a lot to give, and it hurts not to give it! Something dries up inside of you if you don't give when you need to give. There has to be a "flow." You don't have a choice as to whether or not you're going to give! If God called you to be a minister, a provider, then you have to give!

***

When someone does something stupid and they know that it's

stupid, you don't have to announce to them that it's stupid. This is when they really need to be upheld.

***

Always deal with people as though you will have an ongoing relationship. If you have to be tough on someone, try to have something go their way in the future. Try to develop a professional sense by separating your working relationship from your personal relationship. If you have to be hard on someone professionally always extend yourself personally, so that they know that you care for them and theirs.

***

It always helps if there is someone else along when you are doing, saying or thinking something important; just talking about it and experiencing it together makes it more real.

***

There are those who think that tender, loving care (TLC) is the secret of relating redemptively. My own experience says that TLC is important, but FLC is far more important. Let me tell you what FLC is: Focused Listening and Concentration. Good relating isn't you doing most of the talking. You have to listen, and not just to what they're saying, but how they're saying it.

***

I used to walk quite a bit, and our headquarters is located in an area where many prostitutes and drug dealers used to hang out. I'd go out for a walk and prostitutes would approach and say, "You want a date?" They never said anything obscene. I remember stopping and telling them, "No, it's not that you're not nice, but Jesus doesn't want me to do that and He's always watching me." The answer wasn't, "I'm married, therefore I don't do these things" even though that was true. But for me to say "I don't do these things" would be taken by many to mean, "I'm a good guy and you are dirt," and frankly I don't think I'm anybody to talk down to prostitutes or dope dealers or anyone else.

So instead, I would just say, "Jesus doesn't want me to do that; He's always watching me." And the greatest compliment I got was that they started calling me "The Jesus Man." And that's the way I would like to be known. They weren't mean about it. I remember one girl saying something to me, and the other one says, "Oh, he's the one who thinks Jesus is watching Him." And I just like that reputation.

***

How do you behave in somebody else's home? Well, remember it's not your house. For example, if you go to a home and the television is blaring so that you can't talk, you don't have the right to get up and turn it down, nor should you tell someone else to turn it down. Instead, just start talking softer and softer so that they can't hear you. And if they want to hear you, they'll either get a chair and get closer to you or they'll turn down the television set. In other words, you always let each person control their own situation.

Resolve

A lot of people could do things they didn't think they could do after talking to me. Many people mistake the hardest part of a difficult task: it's resolve. Sometimes it was so sad to see people turn away from the things they wanted to do, but were afraid to try. I'd think, if they'd just come alongside, they could see . . .

Responsibility

If you see something wrong, and you don't say something to rectify it, you're wrong. Nowhere does the Bible say that "none of my business" or "don't get involved" are proper approaches. The Bible says you *are* involved and you *must* take responsibility. When you have the power to speak to a situation and you don't speak, you're part of the cause of whatever wrong happens.

Risk Taking

Unless we make the conscious decision to take risks we will change the character of this ministry so that we might as well merge with those who want to do less.

***

We will not know where we are at in the faith until we start taking risks. We need to test our trust, and we need risks to tell us how much the Lord means to us and how strong our faith is.

***

If you want to have gains for God, you must take risks.

Sin

Many sins are sinful because they are out of time, such as premarital sex. In those cases, what is a sin on one day is not a sin on another. Other sins began as acceptable behaviors that become sinful because of excess. Know the boundaries where the status changes from right to wrong.

Teachability

How do you gauge teachability? Is a person teachable because you tell them something and a week later they quote you, showing that they remember what you said? No. That may be the way you get through school, but it's not the way to get through life. While a teachable person might be able to repeat what you said, the way you see she is teachable is that she applied what you said. She tried it, and got back to you to let you know if it did or didn't work.

Teamwork

The main characteristic of a good mission leader is that he or she is a team builder. Not every competent worker or missionary is a team builder, but every team builder is a competent worker in all of the details or tasks to be performed.

***

Many want to build a team, but they don't want to build an individual. You're going to have a good team by building up individuals. You have to have the heart, the vision, the concern for the individual, not the group. The way they function together is the group.

***

If you can be part of building a person's vision and building their work habits—no matter where they go, they'll always be on your team even if they're angry at you.

***

When you're recruiting a team, get different people. Know and appreciate their different strengths. Discover their weaknesses as well as their strengths. If they are otherwise good people, get somebody else to cover their weaknesses.

On a baseball team we have room for a pinch hitter who is likely to knock a home run. He doesn't have to run so fast if he can hit that far. Everybody doesn't have to be the same. Know the differences on your team, and enjoy the differences.

Tension vs Stress

There is a difference between tension and stress. You cannot avoid tension unless you decide you won't allow yourself to feel. You cannot avoid tension unless you also avoid responsibility. To avoid tension is to avoid serving God. We can't avoid tension, but we can avoid stress.

What is the difference? Tension is a tautness, a pulling; stress is a destructive way of dealing with tension. Tension is like a rope that is used to pull a load. Stress is when you get tangled up in the rope, or when the rope becomes frayed or snaps because you are pulling the wrong load or too many loads at once. Don't seek to avoid tension; seek to manage it. We grow by maintaining and managing tension.

To manage tension and avoid stress, keep a leash on each of the things you should pull, but don't try to pull them all at once. You may have your attention on several things, but your tension should be on only one thing. Deal with it in a timely manner. The reason many are stressed is because of a lack of focus on the point of proper tension. What one thing is holding the whole back? Keep the leash on the other things, but relax the tension on them and apply your energy to the one load which is holding you back.

***

An article on missionary tension stated that confrontation is the source of most tension and stress in missionaries. We have more confrontation and stress than most ministries. Much of our stress exists because we don't confront at the right time or in the right way. We need to find creative ways to confront one another to keep our pace and to keep us from avoiding necessary kinds of confrontation.

***

A natural tension exists between people in authority and those under their authority. People in authority are responsible to be in control of maintaining principles and standards. If you relax the reins of control too much, they will break when that natural tension begins pulling again. Some people will avoid tension and thus relinquish their authority. Don't be afraid to lose people over the matter of your authority.

God is in authority over all of us. He has a tension with you, and He's pulling you along.

Theology

All of Scripture, both Old and New Testaments, converge in the person of Christ. It is not that the Old must be read through the New or that the New must be read in light of the Old, but that both Old and New, the entire expanse of God's progressive revelation, converges in the person of Christ.

Time Management

To avoid wasting time, remember what tempts you to waste it—not the things or people you dislike, but the people and things you *do* like. Ration them out. A helpful way to organize is to always do the unpleasant things first. Get it done so you can do the pleasant things last. You'll be surprised how efficiently you'll deal with the unpleasant things. Always begin with the job you like least.

Training

Intelligence is knowing, wisdom is knowing how to apply what you know and applying it properly. We have too many people who are educated and yet are not wise. This is one reason we continue to emphasize training and not just education. Education is only a part of training. Training is teaching people how to use what they know.

Transparency

It annoys a lot of people that I'm so open in discussing your faults and my own faults. Part of love is being open with one another. When I discuss your faults in front of others and in front of you, it's not designed to humiliate. In fact, you can't humiliate a humble person. But it is so that we can all bear things together. Bearing things together is the result of love. That's the way that Jesus loved.

"Mind your own business" is not a Bible motto. The Bible says, "Confess your faults to one another." Why do you suppose you confess your faults to one another? Accountability. Humility. Discipline. Yes, but there's something else.

If you conceal your faults you're saying, "I will never change, this is a permanent state of being. I will always be this way. I'm so rotten and I can't bear the idea that other people should know."

Trust

I've always asked that if something goes wrong that I hear it from the staff member first because if I discover it from someone else I always feel that there's a good possibility that the individual decided to conceal fault from me, hoping that I'd never discover it. That causes trust to evaporate and trust is really essential in the kind of working relationships we have.

Truth

Never reduce a lie to a mere misunderstanding. When you give the correct understanding and someone refuses to hear it, they've chosen to believe an untruth and you have to deal with it just that way. It is our duty to combat illusions and falsehoods that abound and enslave people.

***

Everyone knows how to tell the truth precisely and yet create a misimpression. We have to choose not to do that.

***

Truth is always working, doing and holding the world together. Truth changes us.

***

When we don't have the strength to avoid what is wrong, and to do what is right, we must not sin against the truth and say that there is another truth which is merely personal. Truth is not a servant; it is a master that we either choose to serve or choose to avoid. Let's call selfishness and weakness what it is, even in ourselves, or we will never get a vision for being other-centered, or find the strength to act on behalf of others.

Vulnerability

Why do we tend to depersonalize? Why do we try not to care? Because we don't want to be hurt. If you do not let yourself feel anything about people, you will not feel pain when they let you down. But where you close out pain, you also close out joy.

As an older minister, I have been hurt by many individuals

who have let me down or turned on me. But that is not the half of it . . . it is the tenth of it! The other nine-tenths is that I have been greatly blessed by the people I deal with. There isn't a person at this Council meeting who hasn't hurt me at some time [and perhaps vice versa]. But disappointments don't characterize relationships if you make yourself vulnerable. If you will open up to people, they will bless you. Remember to enjoy those blessings from people to help you endure the pain they also cause you.

* * *

One thing you don't seem to see about relating is something that Y'shua showed you over and over again. It's the value of vulnerability. The "can-do" attitude can keep us from developing the "I need you" sense of vulnerability. It is prideful and works against the formation of community.

Worship

Every moment we should be conscious of the person of the Almighty, His will, His way and how what we're doing at a given moment fits into an eternal program of redemption and reconciliation. The worship of God is not a distraction from life. It is the focus upon the source of life. It is seeing the world refracted through its Creator. It is having the blueprint in front of us with the knowledge of how things are to be done.

But when we talk about seeing God, or seeing the world or ourselves through God, we must confess that we still see through a glass darkly, though one day we shall we know even as we're known. True worship involves a great deal of groping, grappling and sometimes grabbing. Our father Jacob grabbed ahold of the angel. He grappled with the angel. He groped in the dark, but in grabbing he would not let go. Worship is often like that.

We know that the [Hebrew] terms "worship" and "service" are synonymous. Do we do our work for God in a worshipful way?

More lessons to follow: unlike the previous, brief extractions, the following lessons are searchable in the Table of Contents and are therefore not in alphabetical order.

The Benefits of Praise

If it gave no other benefit, the praise of God would still be a most worthy worship endeavor. Nevertheless, aside from the spiritual advantage of enabling us to relate to the Lord in a proper way, praise provides certain psychological benefits in the midst of problems.

Praise helps us avoid depression. Letting our minds dwell on our problems can lead to depression. Depression, in turn, can lead to feelings of hopelessness and helplessness. When we fix our minds on God, who loves and cares for us, we magnify our sense of His presence. Then, though we might still feel weak, our hope is renewed as we consider the One who has been our help.

Praise helps us feel secure. Our troubles often involve failed relationships. People have let us down, or we have disappointed others. When we praise God, we can remember that *He* never fails, and even if we have failed Him, we can be forgiven. A good beginning for a praise session is to extoll our heavenly Father for His faithfulness. By celebrating His faithfulness and resting in it, we become inwardly secure.

Praise helps us gain perspective. Usually when we are thinking about our problems we are not really seeking to solve them, but are involved in self-centered pity. When we let the praise of God fill our minds, we think of *His* worthiness, not ours. Dwelling on the thought that we don't deserve a particular evil that has befallen us, or that we deserve a particular good that has not come our way, only makes us more self-centered and unworthy. Contemplating God's worthiness as we praise Him humbles us and makes us see things in the proper perspective and degree of importance.

Praise helps us appreciate God's greatness. Many think of praise to God as some kind of obsequious flattery whereby God is so pleased that He will do as we ask and grant us our petitions. That would be no more than manipulation. God cannot be flattered into doing what we want. He wants us to contemplate what is real about Him and confess those verities in prayer as we consider them. Worship by praise should never be considered the prologue to pleadings. In the course of prayer anything that can be said without much thought has little value. Part of the purpose of praise is to enable us to discover what is praiseworthy in God.

Praise raises our awareness of God's presence. Some people think the way to praise God is to mouth something over and over again until we have repeated it an acceptable number of times. They think as those in eastern religions do who rotate a prayer wheel. Y'shua said that we should not use vain repetitions, as the heathen do. "For they think they shall be heard for their much speaking." But we are assured that our heavenly Father does hear, and that He knows our needs before we speak them. The prayer pattern given by our Savior is fairly simple, with comparatively few words. When it comes to praise we must be careful to strive for quality rather than quantity. Thoughtful praise is a celebration that raises the level of our awareness of God's own being. No amount of verbiage can do that unless it has focus and progression. True praise comes from events, even if those events are only inward realizations and recollections. True praise brings our hearts (emotions) and our minds (intellect and understanding) to the place where we can view God from a more intimate vantage point.

When we devote ourselves to responding to the situations of life with some word of praise to God for everything that happens, we begin to realize His place, His power, His presence and His purpose, and we acquire a proportionate sense of values as to what is truly important.

SO PRAISE THE LORD ANYHOW, ANYPLACE, ANYWAY!

Calvary: a Dark Image that Sheds Light

Jesus did not use a power image of Himself to impress the world. He said, "If I be lifted up"—meaning, if I be crucified—"I will draw all men to me."

There is something about the impression of death that challenges people to come closer to God, to take a look at stark reality. Considering the pain, the apparent finality, the fearfulness of the event, one might think that images of death would be utterly repellent. And yet, the crucifixion image, this event, has been the object of attracting sinful humanity to the Savior.

There's a saying that you can catch more flies with honey than with vinegar. For those who place great value on accumulating flies, that's great advice. But that which is sweet to sophisticated and sinful persons only has momentary appeal. Stop and think: How long do you savor a candy bar? Now think again: How long do you remember a toothache? All the bright and beautiful things give a momentary impression. But it is often the darker images of pain which press and impress.

That is not to say that we must stand up and scare people with the consequences of sin by describing sinners in the hands of an angry God. I don't believe in unduly frightening people. If you try to frighten people into action, you can also paralyze them by fear so that they are unable to act.

Why is it that Calvary, pain or the dark things draw people in? It goes beyond our basic motivations for food, shelter, reproduction or self-esteem. More than anything else, we want to have meaning and significance in life. There must be a reason for it all that goes beyond this moment of pleasure or this moment of pain. Somehow there is a craving within us that life must mean something. Pain can be endured if it has meaning. And we live to discover meaning.

To understand the meaning of life, we must gaze at death. The image of the cross is not one of passive resignation to accepting pain. That is what the world sees, but they miss the whole point. Calvary was not Jesus' passive resignation to accepting death. Yes, it is a matter of acceptance, but not with resignation. It is the Almighty Son of God defiantly telling sin to do its worst. If you doubt that defiant attitude, think of Y'shua in judgment before Pilate. "Are you the king of the Jews?" Y'shua replied, "You said it!"

When Y'shua cried out, "My God, my God, why have you forsaken me?" it was not a cry of despair, it was a declamation of a psalm that had indicated what was happening. He was denoting the experience of Psalm 22.

In order for an image to work effectively, there has got to be a certain amount of disparity. The kind of image which draws people is not just sweetness and light, but darkly etched events set against a light background.

Common Leadership Problems

Most of you have had leadership failures in dealing with subordinates because

1. You wanted people to like you. You should have wanted them to respect you.
2. You behaved as though you trusted them when the truth of the matter is you were being slack. You weren't aware enough of what they were doing or of their potential.
3. You waited too long to deal with problems.

Here's a principle that I've given you before. Put it in a book of principles. Deal with a problem when a pattern emerges. If somebody is very late one time, you don't have to worry. If the person is late two times, you should be concerned. If he is late a third time, you have to deal with it. Deal with patterns.

When people with a problem pattern really want help, give them help, give them guidance, give them what they need.

You might have to get up at 6:00 in the morning to call the person to see if he's up so he can get in on time. The fact that you care enough to call at 6:00 in the morning is an inspiration for that person to do what's right. In other words let the solution to your subordinate's problem cost you something.

If that doesn't work, make the person wish the problem didn't exist. In other words, see to it that they have enough reason to make sure they don't allow the problem to happen again.

Again, first offer help. Involve yourself; give of yourself; let it cost you something. If that doesn't help, don't be afraid to let the problem cost the other person something at a price they don't want to pay. Both of these things have to be done prayerfully.

WE SHOULD BE PRODUCING THE FRUITS OF THE SPIRIT.

Spiritual Agriculture

When it comes to ministry, cultivation is how we tend to those things—including ourselves, our environment, our families, our friends and those who ought to become our friends—so as to produce growth.

Therefore, the purpose of cultivation is to produce fruit. Now Jesus talked about production. He said that when the vine dresser finds a limb which doesn't produce, he cuts it off. So the unproductive aspects we find in our own lives should be trimmed off to make way for new growth. Nothing grows without pruning.

When we talk about producing, what is it that every believer, every minister ought to be producing? First and foremost we should be producing the fruit of the Spirit. "But the fruit of the Spirit is love, joy, peace, longsuffering, kindness, goodness, faithfulness, gentleness, self-control. Against such there is no law. And those *who are* Christ's have crucified the flesh with its passions and desires. If we live in the Spirit, let us also walk in the Spirit. Let us not become conceited, provoking one another, envying one another" (Galatians 5:22–26).

What people in the world are producing, because of a lack of spiritual cultivation, is the fruit of the flesh. "Now the works of the flesh are evident, which are: adultery, fornication, uncleanness, lewdness, idolatry, sorcery, hatred, contentions, jealousies, outbursts of wrath, selfish ambitions, dissensions, heresies, envy, murders, drunkenness, revelries, and the like; of which I tell you beforehand, just as I also told *you* in time past, that those who practice such things will not inherit the kingdom of God" (Galatians 5:19–21).

It's significant to note that the fruit of the flesh in Galatians 5 precede the fruit of the Spirit. Fruits of the flesh don't need to be cultivated. They're like weeds; they grow up naturally and if left alone, they take over.

What we should be cultivating in our own spiritual life is the fruit of the Spirit. The way we grow spiritually is to abide in the Lord, through the Word of God and through discipline (pruning).

Once we are saved, who we are, what we do, what we count for, our worth, our value is fruit to be cultivated, both through our faithfulness in spiritual disciplines, and through the work of the Holy Spirit.

Cultivation is not limited to what we need to be fruitful in our own spiritual lives. Ministry means cultivating others.

When the farmer commits to raising a crop, he commits himself to supplying other people with a needed product as well as providing for his own family. He uses the ground to bring into existence that which didn't exist before. We have to see ministry in the same way. God is going to use us to bring something into existence that didn't exist before: someone's prayer, someone's joy, someone's witness—we'll be part of something new that's going to happen for them and this involves our commitment.

Though the farmer may have raised a particular crop for many years, each time he plants the seed the outcome is different. Even using the best seed, the yield varies. But he can't abandon the crop even if he knows it will be a low producing yield, he has to see it through to harvest. Now, there's an exception and that's when the crop is ruined by rain or storm. Then he then must count the crop as loss and plow it under. But even the plowing under of the crop makes it into fertilizer for future growth. And this too is part of his commitment.

Once you start sowing seed you need to stay with the field unless God moves you. Do the cultivating and the weeding and you'll experience the joy of the harvest.

Commitment

> 2 Timothy 2:2: "And the things that you have heard from me among many witnesses, commit these to faithful men who will be able to teach others also."

We all think that we know what commitment means. However, a lot of the problems we face as ministers have to do with staying committed to the task—and many of our spiritual problems are due to misunderstanding the nature of commitment. Difficulties with those we supervise stem from problems with their commitment and ours.

Commitment doesn't mean "Do what I say." We should be commanding a lot less and commending a lot more. Here are seven things to remember about the nature of commitment.

• Concentration
Get your mind set. Get your heart set. Take a stand. There are spiritually and morally flimsy people who say they are committed, yet they lack concentration.

Concentration means setting your mind and heart on those areas where it should be. Close out other things. Closing out those other things is a very important part of commitment.

• Conviction
Conviction is confidence in the truth. It is authoritatively standing on what is true. Remember, it isn't our own authority but the authority of the truth. When we stand in our own authority we can crumble.

• Concern
This is not the least of commitment. When someone approaches me with something that I haven't had a chance to ponder, I might not care enough about the situation to respond right away. It takes time to become concerned. When we are committed we learn to care and we are concerned.

• Confession

Confession is saying what is real—telling the truth, including the truth about ourselves. We all have to admit that commitment is a "sometimes" thing with us, not only commitment to the work but also commitment to our Lord. Confession is administering the antidote.

Scripture says if anyone has sinned let him confess his sins. Why? Y'shua said, "And you shall know the truth, and the truth shall make you free." There are people whose lives are a morass because they have so justified their own attitudes and actions that they don't know the truth about themselves. They can't return to what is right because they have convinced themselves that they were never wrong.

We've got to actively say what is real, what is true, what ought or ought not to be. Sometimes we say "I can't" when we mean "I won't." One of the things in confessing sin before God and honestly relating to our commitments is to say, "At this point in my life I'm unwilling; I'm not ready." That will help fasten you into your commitment because you're still headed in the right direction.

• Connection

You join or rejoin the direction of your commitment. You're headed God-ward, and commitment means to connect or reconnect. But there has to be a connection.

• Correction

Correction means viewing and reviewing to see that things line up with the five principles previously mentioned.

• Commission

In a sense this is what we receive and what we give to others when we share our commitment. "Co" means along with. The word *mission* is obvious to everyone. Commission means to go along with the mission. It takes an act of the will. Those who receive a commission are set apart.

Those who understand the nature of commitment are usually the most cautious about making commitments. They know that once they agree, there's a price to be paid and that price can't be renegotiated along the way or one's honor is lost.

A strong desire to do the right thing is not a commitment. Making a commitment is like buying something; if you can't pay the price, you don't declare it to be yours.

Faithfulness

According to 2 Timothy 2:2, we should commit what we have learned to faithful people. How do you know that somebody is faithful? Here are seven signs that indicate faithfulness, and you'll notice an overlap with the signs of commitment.

- **Care**

Faithful people care. They not only care, but they show that they care.

- **Commitment**

Faithful people can commit themselves. There is a type of person who cannot honestly commit himself. This is a person who doesn't have a conscience, or not much of one. Don't burden these people with commitments because you'll only add to your troubles and add to their troubles. Minister to them, but don't let them minister with you. Uphold them as best as you can. These people feel a lot of pain. They don't know the joy of having people love them or really being able to love others.

The faithful person can make and keep commitments. People who are faithful in little things are usually faithful in big things. If a person doesn't care enough about being on time, it doesn't mean he's going to be unfaithful in bigger things, but this might be a clue. Watch how a person handles little things.

- **Conscience**

Watch for the person who is moved by conscience. This is a person who believes in right and wrong and wants things to be right. Do you know anyone like that?

You are leaders in part because you believe that things can be right and you believe that things can be wrong. Right and wrong are not just labels to get something that you want. You don't always believe that you're right. The psychopath will say "up is down" and "down is up" if it serves his purposes. He has a sliding scale of right and wrong depending on what he needs at that moment. But look for people with conscience who are moved by right and wrong.

• **Consistence**
We've all been disappointed by the person who offers to come do music for us. The person promised many things, and the first time, did a pretty good job. But the second time it was less. The third time it was less, and so on. But maybe the seventeenth time it was just right and the person did all the wonderful things he or she promised.

It is better to have someone who can perform on a medium level consistently so people know what to expect. Look for consistent people, not those who raise high expectations that they only occasionally meet.

• **Circumspection**
A faithful person is circumspect. Some of us had to learn our weaknesses through stumbling, and now we walk circumspectly. We avoid those things which cause us to stumble.

• **Contentedness**
The faithful person is content with a reasonable role. Faithfulness is when a person has a good singing voice, enjoys singing, yet is only asked to do a solo occasionally and isn't unhappy about it. He or she is happy to fill the role that is needed.

• **Cooperation**
This quality is not first nor is it last in importance. I recruited many of you through testing. If you were traveling with me, I may have held out my briefcase without saying anything. This was a test to see if you would carry it. Cooperative means that the person operates with you. Don't expect anyone to cooperate with you unless you are cooperative with them. It is a mutual thing. You submit to one another. And you commit to one another's concerns.

Dealing with Fear

There is a difference between ungodly fear and Christian concern. Ungodly fear—the emotion produced and/or utilized by Satan—enervates. It dulls our awareness. It makes us "react" to problems that may never even arise. It robs us of peace, replacing it with worry. It robs us of productivity, channeling our energies into jousting at windmills. It robs us of relationships, focusing our time and attentions on overwhelming concern. Finally, it robs us of God's blessings as we try to deal with real or imagined problems in our own strength.

God answers the problems posed by anxieties with one word: *trust!* Trust is a decision. It involves taking a stand, remembering that commitment, and behaving accordingly. It means that in the midst of an anxiety attack, we must call upon God, our Defender and Advocate, who just "happens" also to be in control of the universe.

Faith and trust are inextricably bound, and you cannot have one without the other. Commitment activates the faith/trust antidote to anxiety. At first an anxious person's commitment to trust may be feeble and bring only momentary relief. But increasingly applied, it will grow in strength and duration.

Some Pointers on Applying Faith/Trust in God

• Affirm and confess that God is.

• Remember that God rewards those who diligently seek Him (Hebrews 11:6).

• Take a stand that God is good, that He loves you, and that He will not let any test befall you that He will not give you the strength to overcome (1 Corinthians 10:13).

- Feed your faith with frequent Scripture readings, memorizing the "trust" passages. A favorite that comes to mind is Isaiah 26:3: "You will keep him in perfect peace, whose mind is stayed on You, because he trusts in You." Don't be afraid to say the verse out loud often and ponder its meaning.

- Resist Satan. Remember that he wants to besiege you with a spirit of fear in order to destroy your victory as a child of God. Declare that your fear is inspired by the enemy and that Christ has defeated him at Calvary (Ephesians 1:20, 21; Colossians 2:15).

- Remember that perfect love casts out fear (1 John 4:18). God's perfect love that culminated at Calvary banishes Satan's power and his arsenal of accusations against the child of God. It is not our love for God, but *His* love for us that accomplishes this.

The most important thing an anxious child of God can do is make a reality check. The evil one would have us believe that the forces arrayed against us are invincible. But remember: his power is limited.

God Himself is our Defense and our Defender. When we take shelter in Him, truly we have nothing to fear but fear itself.

Spiritual Swordsmanship

The Bible speaks of itself, of the Word of God, as a sword. One good thing about this sword: it doesn't bring death; it brings life. Death has already been conquered through Y'shua. The sword that we have is a sword to be used to knight people, to make them noble, to make them part of the royal family. But when you go out with a sword, any sword, you become a threat.

If you were standing on a bloody, ancient battlefield, how could you tell the winners from the losers when the battle was over? You can tell by who still has a sword. The sword is a symbol of authority. The apostle Paul uses it that way in the book of Romans to talk about civil authority: "He doesn't bear the sword in vain."

Likewise, our swords are not that we are ordained as ministers or employed by Jews for Jesus, but our sword is the Word of God: the sword that we're under as well as the one we use. As I found out early on, and as all of you have found out, it's not particularly the ministers, the seminary graduates or the professors who know the Word of God well. Why? Because just about the point at which you think these are the beholders of knowledge, you're going to meet some elderly woman who doesn't know a thing about Hebrew or Greek, but she's got that Book down, and she can tell you the what's what and the who's who and the when's when. And I want to tell you that when she wields this Book, she has more spiritual authority than you do, because the Book itself is God's authority.

MANY PEOPLE ARE ADDING TO WHAT THEY HAVE BUT SUBTRACTING FROM WHAT THEY ARE.

Value Judgments: What Is the Basis for "Ought" and "Ought Not"?

Assessments or pronouncements that attribute goodness or some degree of goodness to things or ideas are called "value judgments."

In our secular society, value judgments are often regarded as an offense. Most people would like to believe that good is whatever seems right to them. This is not a new way of thinking.

At the dawn of modern thought Hobbes and Spinoza advanced the idea that "good" is merely the name we give something that we happen to desire or like. Therefore, good is not a discoverable property of things themselves. Hume added that it is impossible to validate any value judgment. This has led to a doctrine—and it is extremely important to see that it *is* a doctrine in today's society. The name of the doctrine is "non-cognitive ethics."

Non-cognitive ethics teaches that we cannot know if statements that assert an "ought" or "ought not" are true or false. A non-cognitive system of ethics rejects absolute values; it presumes that we cannot know that something is really right or wrong, good or bad. Non-cognitive ethics regards value judgments as nothing more than an expression of one's own likes or dislikes, desires or aversions. Right and wrong are relative to each individual. Therefore, the question in non-cognitive ethics is, "Does this seem good to me?"

How do we show that values are *not* merely relative to our own perceptions?

This brings us into the realm of "prescriptive" vs "descriptive" values, or "ought" vs "is."

1. A **descriptive** statement is: "More people will like you if you are kind than if you are cruel." This describes a reality. You can tell if it is true or false by measuring how people respond to kindness and how they respond to cruelty. You can measure it against reality and if it corresponds, it is true.

2. A **prescriptive** statement is: "People ought to be kind." This is a prescription for the way people should behave which stands alone as an idea. In what way can you tell if it is true or false? What can you measure an idea against? How can we know the truth about what ought to be, if truth relates to the way things are, while ought is an idea?

3. An understanding that truth includes more than descriptive statements thus becomes the turning point in establishing that there are objective value judgments.

Aristotle suggested prescriptive statements are true if they conform to what he called "right desire." He did not say what he meant by "right desire." But if a desire can be right, then it is what we *ought* to desire. So we distinguish between what we ought to desire and what we simply desire whether or not we ought to. That's the difference between real and apparent good. (Something *appears* good to us just by virtue of our desire. Only those things which are right for us to desire are truly good.)

The goods we desire are either possessions (external) or perfections (personal). The latter increase or amplify our very being by actualizing our potential. Many people find that the quality of their life diminishes even though they are accumulating more and more goods, and they don't know why. They are adding to what they have, but they are subtracting from what they are.

The whole idea of rejecting standards of absolute right and wrong did not begin with the sophists, Hobbs, Spinoza or Hume. It began in the Garden of Eden, when Eve accepted the proposition that an action that God warned would be wrong . . . might actually be right for her. And ever since, the human race has been rebelling against the idea that God is always right and whenever we disobey Him, we are wrong. Scripture does have something to say about this, and that is, "There is a way that seems right to man, but the end thereof is death."

When people say that "ought" or "ought not" are simply

collections of what seems good to us, they are making a statement about God—either that He does not exist or that His existence is not relevant to us.

We are to imitate God's character and obey His commands. We cannot separate His character from His commands or vice versa. Who He is and what He wants us to do are two sides of the same coin. We need to ascribe equal value to being and to doing what God's character and commands require us to be and do.

Why Witness to Jewish People?

Until recently, evangelical Christians didn't have to think twice about Jewish evangelism. Evangelical churches realized the urgent need to present the gospel to all people so that others might gain God's forgiveness and eternity in heaven. It was understood that "all people" included Jewish people.

Now there is considerable deviation from the understanding that Jesus is the only way to salvation. Nowhere is this seen more clearly than in the attitudes of many churches toward Jewish evangelism. Some question whether or not the Jewish people need the gospel at all. Others say that Jews need Jesus, but they challenge just about any method of evangelism that doesn't begin with a Jewish person approaching a Christian to know more about Christ. Usually there has not been firsthand observation of the methods that are challenged or rejected.*

Why has Jewish evangelism become so controversial? Two reasons present themselves. One is the all-too-human tendency to choose the easy path. It's easy to go with the flow—to evangelize those who are down and out, who have no cultural barriers to prevent them from hearing our message. Jewish people are among the people groups missiologists have described as "gospel resistant." Jews who feel a need to resist Jesus tend to see Him as a threat to the survival of the Jewish community. They do not realize that our survival does not depend on submitting to the religion of Judaism, but to the God of Abraham, Isaac and Jacob. Anyone who wishes to take the path of least resistance will avoid witnessing to Jews.

---

*We understand that some Jewish community leaders may feel justified in saying or repeating things about our [missionary] motives or methods that cannot be substantiated in order to protect Jewish people from what they see as a threat. However, it is most discouraging when Christians hear and repeat portions of these accusations or otherwise draw negative conclusions without checking with their own brothers and sisters in Christ to see if they are true.

The other reason is that many Christians—whether or not they realize or admit it—want to be "politically correct." Maybe the second is just part of the first.

Most describe their inactivity in noble or compassionate terms. One says, "I don't target Jews. I preach the gospel to everyone who comes to my meetings." Another says, "Yes, Jews need the gospel, but they are so hurt by the Holocaust and other persecutions that we have no right to speak at this time."

Christians need to recognize that it takes courage to witness to someone who just might be offended, angry or argumentative. It takes courage to broach the subject to someone who may not only reject your message, but reject you for telling it. A person who is not willing to do that sometimes finds it easier to come to terms with their own choices by putting down those who *are* willing to be rejected when they ought to be praying for and encouraging them for doing the difficult thing.

Some who want to be politically correct say, "The Jews have their own religion, an ancient and noble religion that predates Christianity." Yes, the Jewish people do have their own religion, and originally it was based entirely on Scripture.

Yet if the Jewish religion were sufficient in itself, why would the all-wise, all-knowing, Son of God tell a religious Jew like Nicodemus, "You must be born again"? Why did God decide that Y'shua (Jesus) should be born to a Jewish mother in a Jewish place in accordance with the Jewish prophets? If the Jews didn't need Jesus, wouldn't it have been better just have Him born in Norway, Karachi, or Papua New Guinea, to those who did need Him?

But God demonstrated—not only through Scripture, but also by the Incarnation at Bethlehem—that if anyone needs Jesus, the Jewish people do. Jewish evangelism is important to God because He cares for the Jewish people and wants them to be reconciled to Him. It's not that one person's religion is superior to another's. Religion is not enough without the reality of the Redeemer.

It is incumbent on the church to continue to evangelize Jewish people because, like everyone else, without Christ, they are lost. Furthermore, Jewish evangelism is almost as important to the church as it is to those unbelieving Jews who need salvation!

The church proves its confidence in the validity of Jesus by earnestly endeavoring to tell all people about the gospel, regardless of what non-Christian religion they possess. If Christians decline to contend for the faith by remaining mute because of someone's religious background, we have basically assented to the world's supposition that biblical Christianity is merely another man-made religion.

Seeing the gospel of Christ as "our religion" is a trap! Those who don't know Christ quite naturally say that we are arrogant to suppose that "our religion" is The Truth. No Christian wants to be arrogant, and many shrivel at the accusation. But let's not confuse confidence and arrogance. We would be arrogant if we had invented the Bible, if we forged a "myth" that Christ was born in accord with the Jewish prophets to be the Jewish Messiah who would do miracles, die for our sins and rise again. But Christianity is not a Gentile invention nor is it a Jewish myth. It is the truth of God, the Creator of the universe.

I have said it before, and I will continue to say it: Bringing the gospel to the Jewish people is perhaps the most significant issue on which the church will prove its character, conviction and commitment to evangelism in general.

THAT'S JUST MOISHE...

Little Sayings

Moishe knew the value of pithy sayings to make a point. Here you'll find some aphorisms he wrote, including favorites from *The Sayings of Chairman Moishe*. Many are full of the folksy flavor that was part of Moishe's upbringing.* In addition, you'll find "one-liners" from his leadership and training lectures—not as catchy, but worth noting. These little sayings may not impart a lot that's new, but they give that fresh zing to help us remember what's important.

Some (though not all) of these sayings impart Moishe's sense of whimsy. We're celebrating that side of Moishe with selected cartoons from our newsletter and some illustrations from *The Sayings of Chairman Moishe*. The cartoons and illustrations underscore an often repeated little saying of Moishe's: "We take the gospel seriously, but we don't take ourselves too seriously."

**The Sayings of Chairman Moishe*, released in the 1970s, is out of print. So far as we know, the sayings taken from that book are original; however a few are "Rosen's take" on a similar saying. Others will sound familiar to you if you've read Moishe's biography, since each chapter began with a little saying. And finally, a few of these little sayings are from Lessons (part 2). Their stand-alone status in this final section makes them easier to find, quote, tweet or otherwise share if you are so inclined. (Please be sure to credit the quotes to Moishe Rosen, and if you share in print, please also mention the copyright on this book.)

Anger

When we shoot the gun of anger we can be killed by the recoil.

Beauty

God put roses on bushes instead of trees so we might stoop to their beauty.

Damage control

When you've got trouble, deal with the troubling facts and make them right before they become a crisis.

***

Unethical conduct aimed at preventing a problem from becoming a crisis will precipitate a crisis.

Death

If we live for Christ, then dying will be easier.

Diligence

Most heroes are stubborn, foolish people who didn't know when to quit.

***

There is no such thing as a hopeless situation. It seems insoluble because people have grown weary of trying.

Enduring

There's no such thing as a comfortable cross.

***

There can be no victory without a battle.

Excuses

The morally crippled use excuses for crutches.

Fun

When you plan to have fun it often backfires; when you work hard, fun is spontaneous.

Humility

Y'shua didn't teach us the right way to wear a crown; He taught us the right way to use a washrag.

***

It is better to give than to receive but it's harder to be a gracious recipient than a gracious giver.

***

The choice is whether you want to do as much as you can or whether you want credit for what you do.

Integrity

Don't ask a man for a vow; if he has integrity that's enough. If he lacks integrity, no vow can bind him.

Keep It in Perspective

Don't think a goose clumsy by its walk—watch it fly.

***

All colors look bright when you have enough light.

***

The difference between what you want and what you need is the same as the difference between what you think and what God thinks.

***

The mistake most of us make in evaluating people is that we try to see what they can be for us and to us instead of trying to see what they can be for God.

***

When people agree with us, we admire their resolve. When they don't, we remark about their stubbornness.

***

It's not so bad to go out on a limb if Christ is the branch

Before you jump on the bandwagon, remember, the tune can change.

***

Nothing is as good as it looks and nothing is as bad as it seems.

***

While we learn from the past, we must be careful not to live in the past.

***

It's not so bad to be out on a limb if Christ is the branch.

Learning

Education furnishes the intellect and training furnishes the ability.

***

Experience is the best teacher; but if you can accept it secondhand, the tuition is less.

***

Wisdom is knowing what to do with what you know.

***

If any of us have finished learning, we've become obsolete.

***

A lot of people in a rut are fully convinced it's their groove.

Listening

We've got all the right answers, but we didn't hear the question.

***

The right answer to the wrong question is worse than no answer at all.

***

Storytelling is a great skill, but not as good as listening.

THE HEART SPEAKS A LANGUAGE THE MOUTH CAN NEVER LEARN.

Love

Love is not lazy, it is always at work.

***

Love has to be shown in order to be known.

***

Love regulated by another person's response is no love at all.

***

The heart speaks a language the mouth can never learn.

***

"For God so loved the world"—anyway!

***

People are hollow because they won't open up enough to let anything in.

Maturity

Children cry over spilled milk; adults wipe it up and pour some more.

***

Maturity is not measured by years but according to how we are able to handle our experiences.

Minimalism

Many people are minimalists. They're unwilling to spend more of themselves than they have to, and as a result, an already small soul shrivels.

***

When we look within and measure our own abilities, we tend to become minimalists, but when we look above and beyond, we gain the vision of what God will enable us to do if we step out in faith.

***

Most of us want to be protected from our own laziness.

***

If we take a shortcut that is not honoring to God, it is no shortcut; it is an undercut.

Ministry

Ministry is not a means of earning a living; it is a way of life.

Miscellaneous

People who live in glass houses shouldn't.

***

There is no contradiction between true science properly researched and the Bible properly interpreted—except in the minds of people who don't understand either.

***

A careful artist doesn't need a big brush.

***

If money can't buy it, it's probably worth having.

***

Since his death, Lenin has come to believe that God exists.

***

Do you ever have the feeling the TV is watching you?

Moderation

Too much of a good thing always leaves something out—the ability to enjoy.

Morality

God does not regard any act or attitude as being inconsequential.

***

The folly of democracy is that we expect our politicians and statesmen to have more principles than the rest of us.

***

People are clever enough to be successful thieves—if only God would turn His back for a few minutes.

***

If we wanted to end all pollution on this planet, humanity would have to vacate.

***

I would rather limp with God than leap with the devil.

Opposition

The right enemies help more than the wrong friends.

***

Be kind to your enemies. They'll worry themselves sick trying to understand your scheme.

***

Every knock is a boost.

Pain and Suffering

Sorrow isn't the enemy of joy; we can feel both at the same time.

***

Suffering is a forge in which God makes saints strong.

Patience

Patience is the virtue we want most for those around us.

***

The man who knows he's going to live for eternity can afford to be patient.

***

Patience is always a choice.

Persecution (for Christ's Sake)

We caught a case of Christ, and we are spreading it—so we've been put into quarantine.

***

You are no one until you are hated by someone for Jesus.

***

If we are hated because of Jesus, we are blessed; if Jesus is hated because of us, woe to us.

Power

God has not given us the power to get what we want; He has given us the power to get what *He* wants.

***

Power is ability. Ability is organized energy.

Prayer

The quality of your prayer shows the quality of your care.

***

Sometimes prayer is just being quiet in the presence of God—the same way that you'd sit with someone you like and appreciate.

***

Reading Scripture is a kind of prayer; it's listening to God, hearing what He wants you to know.

Prejudice

Jesus is the door in the wall of prejudice.

Principles

Character is built on principles and policies and not on appearances and melodies.

Religion

Religion is not enough without the reality of the Redeemer.

***

The quality of your life is shaped by what you really believe, not just what you say you believe.

***

Thou shalt not give commandments (unless you're God).

***

Christianity is the best Jewish enterprise.

Responding to Insults

You have to decide whether you want to get a pound of flesh or get a point across.

Selfishness

The man all wrapped up in himself is a mighty small package.

***

A man who lives for himself has a very small reason for living.

Sermons

The worst sin of preachers is boring people, because it gives the Almighty a bad reputation.

***

If you want to teach people not to listen, state the obvious over and over again.

***

If you want to compliment a preacher, don't say how much you enjoyed the sermon; say how you will change as a result of hearing it.

***

Stop talking before people stop listening.

Spiritual Birth

A person born in a Christian home isn't necessarily a Christian any more than a person born in a bakery is a bagel.

***

If being born didn't give much satisfaction, try being born again.

Stewardship

If someone wants to build castles in the sky, that's their business, but don't you pay the rent for them.

***

Do not defend what is not attacked.

***

Do not buy more than you can use or easily store.

***

The cheapest price is not always a good reason to buy.

***

The highest price doesn't mean the highest quality.

***

Always use fewer people than you think you need.

Temptation

No one is a saint until, knowing sin gives exquisite pleasure, he chooses to avoid it.

Traditions

Traditions can be helpful or harmful; some traditions obscure what they intend to affirm.

Truth

Never deny the truth because of your inability to imagine it.

* * *

The truth exists neither to aid us nor to oppose us.

* * *

A PERSON BORN IN A CHRISTIAN HOME ISN'T NECESSARILY A CHRISTIAN ANY MORE THAN A PERSON BORN IN A BAKERY IS A BAGEL.

The truth is never cheap, but the righteous can always afford it.

***

Once you discover a person has lied, don't think that's the only lie they ever told you or will tell you.

Unity

We're part of the vine; we must hang together.

What's Important

Anyone deserves five minutes of my time.

Witnessing

I always knew there was one person that I should preach to, but didn't know who it was, so I preached to them all.

***

It is not arrogant to put our confidence in Jesus or to urge others to consider Him; it would be arrogant for us to behave as though He is merely "our religion."

***

Careless Christians vaccinate their friends against the gospel. They give them just enough of a dose that they never catch a case.

***

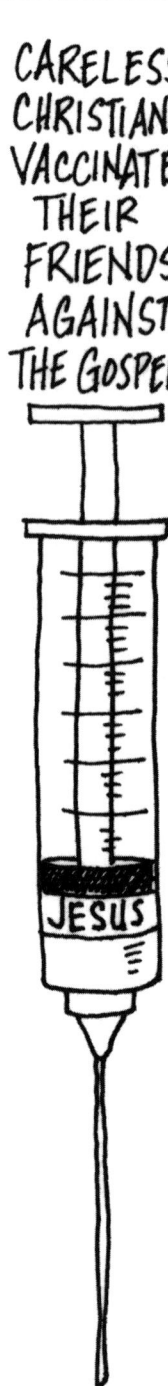

In the case of Christianity, the evidence is being delivered.

***

The Jewish people are God's chosen messengers, but most Jews haven't yet received the message.

***

Bringing the gospel to the Jewish people is perhaps the most significant issue on which the church will prove its character, conviction and commitment to the gospel.

***

The church needs to preach the gospel to the Jews so that eventually the Jews can preach the gospel to the world!

THE **CHURCH** NEEDS TO PREACH THE GOSPEL TO THE **JEWS**...

SO THAT EVENTUALLY THE JEWS CAN PREACH THE GOSPEL TO THE **WORLD**.